TOWARD THE MYSTERY

William Edelen

For Craig
with much
respect
Bill Edelen

JOSLYN-MORRIS, Publishers
120 S. 3rd
Boise, Idaho 83707

ABOUT THE COVER

We have a very special and sacred place, my wife and I. It is a little rustic cabin that goes back to the turn of the century. We call it Maka Wakan, which is the Oglala Sioux name for 'the Sacred Earth.'

One magical spring morning I decided to round up old, rusty scrap iron from our land, some buried deep in dried grass, and create a Tai Chi disk for the front of our cabin. The parts presented themselves easily as the living Tao was at work, in harmony with the morning's venture. The North American Indian would understand the Tao. They lived with the Tao. They called it Wakan. It is the same.

It is a very, very special place, Maka Wakan. There is an energy there. There is a healing there. "The galling harness of civilization drops away" . . . and the Mystery reminds all who visit there to 'consider the flowers of the field and the birds of the air, that they toil not, neither do they spin;' the Osprey and the Indian paint brush, the Eagle and the wild daisies, a hovering hawk, riding the wind, and Trillium. It is a special place, Maka Wakan. "There is only time . . . and the river flowing."

For . . . Elizabeth Geraldine Edelen . . .
my wife . . . known as Jerry
long before my eyes saw you . . .
my spirit knew you . . .

Acknowledgements

I want to thank the publisher and editorial staff of THE IDAHO STATESMAN for their contribution to this presentation of columns. I would also like to express my gratitude to the following persons who through their encouragement and support made this book a possibility; The Corydon Wagner Foundation of Tacoma, Washington, Mrs. Warren (Jayne) Brown, Carl Shaver, James Hait, Mrs. Frank (Lydia) Edwards, Nelle Tobias, Herman Stelling, and members of the First Congregational Church of Tacoma, Washington, and to Ward Hower who spent hours in his law office tying together all of the loose ends.

What can I say to artist Julie Wawirka, who on the faith that this book was a contribution to free spirits and open minds, gave hours of her time producing the beautiful and significant art work. Dear Julie, thank you. And remembering the contribution to my life of three special people, my mother, still living in Oklahoma City and on a continual spiritual quest; my father, who long ago went on to experience other dimensions of the Mystery, but is not forgotten by his son; and sister Ilva who never lets me get away with falling back into sexist, male-oriented language.

Dorothy Carter, how wonderful you were to give so many tedious hours to proofreading.

Esther Binning, I just wanted to get your name in here because in your 86th year you are still giving such beautiful music, as our church organist, to us all.

And Samantha I wanted to thank you for many things, especially loving our dogs.

For grandson Matthew, who refers to me only, as "the Man," and grand-daughters Kimberly and Donnella.

And to my wife, Jerry, who said to me about a dozen times in that firm voice that means business, "those columns ARE going to be published" and a final "thank you" to Larry Morris, of Joslyn-Morris, who said the same words. "Those columns ARE going to be published and my company is going to do it."

Table of Contents

Introduction

It was a hot, steamy summer July day in 1981, when in blue jeans and sweat shirt, I found myself sitting opposite a lovely, cool young lady editor named Julie Titone at THE IDAHO STATESMAN. For several years I had written a regular monthly column for the nationally distributed magazine *The Congregationalist.* Having barely unpacked in McCall I headed for Boise and THE IDAHO STATESMAN to see if I could stir up any interest in a similar column. That is where it all started. After listening carefully, she said "we will talk about it and let you know." I left thinking this was one of those "don't call us, we will call you" things. Several weeks later the phone rang and there was Julie on the other end saying "we're going to do it . . . start writing them, and you are free to pursue subject material any way you wish."

For two years now THE IDAHO STATESMAN has provided a free flowing religious forum that is unique and rare for a Saturday "religion" or "church" page. In most newspapers it is the dullest page of the week, with a few church announcements or bland, cliche-filled articles picked off the wire service.

We are living in a time when we are inundated, through television, radio and magazines, by the fundamentalist, evangelical, "born again" religious voice. These columns, and this book, offer an intelligent alternative; another option. I have lost count of the letters that have said: "thank you for bringing in so much fresh air," "how refreshing it is to hear a minister speak to the questions that I have always asked . . . and everyone avoided." One woman wrote: "In high school I asked my minister to explain the Trinity. I told him it made no sense at all to me. He just patted me on the head, in a condescending way, and said "some day, when you are grown you will understand it. Well. I am grown and I still do not understand it." This letter from an Idaho Lutheran minister: "Thank you for helping some of us ministers come out of the closet and discuss things from the pulpit that we have been afraid to face."

These columns have been written for minds that are not afraid to question, and for those free spirits who realize that religious beliefs can be examined by the same critical and objective eye as any other belief system. If you feel that Christianity, and religion is saturated still with witchcraft, magic and superstition, then you will receive much from this book. It is my firm belief that religious creeds and dogma have no place in the world we live in. They are a violation to the free mind and spirit of human beings.

"I have sworn upon the altar of God eternal hostility against every tyranny over the mind of man" wrote Thomas Jefferson. No tyranny can so bind human minds in chains as religious tyranny. This book of columns is for those brave enough to examine the chains. The reward for such an examination is freedom; freedom to pursue the religious quest in your own way, guided only by your own insights, your own feelings and your very own intuition, as you point your life toward the Source . . . and toward . . . the Mystery.

William Edelen
at Maka Wakan
in The Moon Of The
Falling Leaves
McCall, Idaho
1983

"Wherever this man has been . . . THERE HAS BEEN NO PEACE . . . but there has been a far, far more significant happening. There HAS BEEN GROWTH . . . on the part of individuals and institutions."
– The President of Valparaiso
University (Indiana)
introducing Dr. Robert Hutchins

"What most of us need is the truth and facts . . . NO MATTER HOW PAINFUL OR DISTASTEFUL. In fact, WE SHOULD PAY ONLY THOSE PEOPLE WHO ARE WILLING TO TELL US THINGS WE DO NOT LIKE TO HEAR . . . IF IT IS FACTUAL. We have no need of the others. Until such time . . . we are STILL CHILDREN."
– Sydney Harris

"Where were you when I laid the foundation of the earth . . . tell me if you have understanding."

— God, to Job

"On the most <u>vital</u> questions . . . science does not even produce evidence."
— Dr. Vannevar Bush

"We must repudiate our modern idolatry of science and technology . . . and dethrone them from the exaggerated pedestals on which we set them."
— Julian Huxley

"The word 'progress' has become totally corrupted."
— Rene Dubos

"Without the ability to rise above scientific expression . . . man will be consumed by a monster in his own brain."
— Dr. Loren Eiseley, anthropologist

"Present-day Americans are not one bit happier (probably less so) than the Indians who inhabited this continent when the first white man stepped on these shores."
— Albert Einstein

"The white man here . . . they are all mad . . . always wanting something . . . always wanting more . . . they are mad, we think."
— Holy man of the Taos Pueblo to
Carl Jung

THE GALAXIES

The population of the universe has been estimated at ONE HUN-
DRED BILLION major galaxies and the universe is still said to be
expanding and evolving. The Mystery behind all of this wonder can
only be called incomprehensible to the human mind. It can only be
called . . . the Mystery.

We can say: "In the beginning . . . God" . . . or in the words of the
Rig-Veda, in the Hymn of Creation: "The flow of Creation, from where
it did arise, He, the Observer, in the highest heaven, He alone knows,
unless . . . He knows it not." The . . . Mystery!

THE SACRED CREATION

"A generation goes, and a generation comes, but the earth remains forever. The sun rises and the sun goes down and hastens to the place where it rises. The wind blows to the south, and goes round to the north, round and round goes the wind, and on its circuits the wind returns. All streams run to the sea, but the sea is not full; to the place where the streams flow, there they flow again . . ."

— Ecclesiastes

"When I consider the heavens, the work of thy fingers, the moon and the stars, which thou hast ordained; What is man . . . that thou art mindful of him?"

— Psalm 8

Every Living Thing Is Sacred
As God's Creation

There is a belief held by many that I have always found to be especially pitiable. It is the idea that only man (Homo sapiens) is spiritual, sacred and made in the image of God. Many want to differentiate between the supernatural and the natural, the sacred and the profane. But if the creation is the work of an omnipotent mystery, then the entire cosmos is its revelation, and everything, sum total, is natural, sacred and spiritual and reflects the image of that same mystery.

"How we delude ourselves," wrote Albert Schweitzer, "if we think otherwise. When we consider the immensity of the universe, we must confess that man is insignificant. Man's life can hardly be considered the goal of the universe. Its margin of existence is always so precarious. A man is ethical only when he considers every living cell, whether plant or animal, sacred and divine."

Dr. Lewis Thomas, head of New York's Memorial Sloan Kettering research center, said, "Every living thing is alive thanks to the living of everything else. Every form of life is connected. The planet Earth is like a single cell. Homo sapiens is really a very immature and ignorant species in the horrible way it has treated all other living organisms."

"The Earth and myself are of one mind," declared Chief Joseph, recognizing the sacredness of all things, every rock, animal and plant. "We are all made from the same elements. We are all manifestations of the mystery. From the common fund came Homo sapiens. From that same fund, and the same material came every other living organism. The little chipmunk is of the same dust as we, and he breathes the same wind and drinks of the same waters. His days are warmed by the same sun and his little heart pulses just like ours . . . and was created by the same First Fountain."

This view of reality, of the oneness of everything, long held by native peoples and Eastern sages, is today being confirmed by physicists and astronomers. "The universe is everything; both living and inanimate things, both atoms and galaxies, and if the spiritual exists, the spiritual and material are one, for the universe is the totality of all things," wrote Fred Hoyle in *Frontiers of Astronomy.*

Einstein once remarked that among all peoples, a 12-year old Hopi child was best prepared to grasp his "Theory of Relativity." The Hopi have no expression for time, either past or future. Time for them is only circulating space where past, present and future are always together as one. Behind and beyond our senses lies a plane of consciousness in which all is related and all is one, and all is now. Everything is united in the mystery, as one, the energy of the sun dancing in a wood-burning

11

fire; a cucumber cucumbering; a flight of geese honking into a north wind; a rising tide crashing and breaking against a resisting beach; or a wild stallion, with nostrils bugling the pride of the free, racing to his mare; mist covering, with affection, hemlock and pine; a cougar stalking a fresh spore on a mountain trail; it is all one and all natural and all sacred and all divine . . . and all revealed images of the "great mystery" behind it all.

"We are the children of this beautiful planet that we have lately seen photographed from the moon," wrote Joseph Campbell. "We were not delivered into it by some god, but have come forth from it. And the Earth, together with the sun, this light around which it flies like a moth, came forth from a nebula; and that nebula, in turn, from space. So that we are the mind, ultimately, of space, each in his own way at one with all, and with no horizons."

Even life and death are one. Life is only a short episode between two mysteries which are yet one. Spring begins with winter, and death begins with birth. We all share the same breath together in this short episode, the trees, the birds, the animals and the human. We dance to a common rhythm.

The interval of life is a mystery between two greater mysteries which are yet one in a universe where all is natural, sacred, an image of God.

"The greatest beauty is organic wholeness,
The wholeness of life and things,
The divine beauty of the universe,
Love that . . . not man apart from that . . ."

– Robinson Jeffers

Other Cultures Reveal Sacredness Of Words, Truth

The distinguished author and poet Robert Penn Warren has just completed an epic poem that he has been working on since 1935. In this Moon of The New Grass it was finally released. It is *Chief Joseph of the Nez Perce*, who called themselves the Nimipu, "The Real People." What a noble self-image. "Real: genuine, not artificial or counterfeit, representing reality and corresponding to what is true."

In my university class, I used to teach the living "religion" of the North American Indian along with the other great religious traditions. That is where it belongs. It was, and is, profound in its comprehension of experience, reality and truth. The word religion was not even in their vocabulary. Everything had a sacred significance and was a reflection of "Wakan" — "The Holy Mystery."

They were centuries ahead of our contemporary theoretical physicists in that they never differentiated between animate and inanimate. Everything was alive with a spirit, every rock and tree, every leaf and blade of grass. Their religion was a design in harmony. Everything and all is interrelated and a part of the whole. As one said for all: "We do not believe our religion, we dance it."

One of their most moving concepts was the sacredness of the word. Words were not to be used lightly, falsely or irresponsibly. This is why the lies and misrepresentations of the whites were so incomprehensible to them. Words were to be used with great reverence and with care. The breath was identified with life itself. The breath, carrying the word, comes from the center of our being, next to the heart; therefore, it imposes a great responsibility upon the person to use words truthfully and carefully.

Would that we today could recapture this beautiful concept, especially those parasites who feed on others through gossip. It is a concept that Jesus was well aware of: "Hear me, all of you; there is nothing outside a man which by going into him can defile him; but the things which come out of the mouth of a man are what defile him." (*Mark 7:14*)

They understood the implications and the significance of our word ecology before we even had it in our vocabulary. Our destruction of the earth, the slaughter of the buffalo for sport, the pollution of our waters and the air we breathe was not only totally repugnant, but sacrilegious, irreverent and a great sin against our mother Earth and the holy.

Vine Deloria, a professor at the University of Arizona and an Oglala Sioux, writes of a non-Indian friend telling him one day what great "progress" the whites had made since they took over the land.

"What did you do with the land when you had it?" he asked. "My mind turned to the Cuyahoga River running through Cleveland that became inflammable due to all of the combustible pollutants dumped into it, and I answered him, 'Perhaps you whites have done things with the land we Indians could never do. How many Indians could have thought of creating an inflammable river?'"

The eminent historian of religions and civilizations, Arnold Toynbee, wrote the following in the *New York Times* on September 16, 1973, in one of his last articles before his death: "For pre-(Christian) man, nature was not a treasure trove of 'natural resources.' Nature was a godess, 'mother Earth,' and the vegetation that sprang from the surface, the animals that roamed and the minerals hiding in the bowels all shared of nature's divinity and were sacred. I have become aware of a startling and disturbing truth, that a new view, monotheism, enunciated in the book of *Genesis*, removed those restraints of awe that precluded greed. Any greedy impulse to exploit nature was held in check by an awe of the sacredness of nature. This inhibition was removed in *Genesis*." (Where we are told "to subdue" the Earth. "Subdue" in Hebrew means to seduce, to conquer and vanquish.)

"For the Indian, to bring his life, outward and inward, into harmony with that of all nature is in essence the meaning of the SACRED SMOKE which arises from the pipe . . . whose bowl is an altar . . . and whose stem is in the BREATH'S PASSAGE. The smoke, the breath, rises into the wind, to unite in harmony with the universe . . . and join this individual with 'wakan' . . . the Great Mystery."
    – *Hartley Burr Alexander*

"The smoke is a breath of prayer."
    – *Black Elk, Sioux Holy Man*

Jesus Would Be Uncomfortable
With "Religion" Today

It was one of those glorious days, in this Moon When The Ponies Shed. Here at 5,000 feet there is a special intense blueness to a sky uncluttered by haze or smog. It was a day "like wine," as they say.

Aspen buds were swelling. The trillium was in bloom and hummingbirds had returned. Walking on such a day is a spiritual experience, when in silence you feel, smell, hear, see, touch and taste, everywhere, the Mystery.

Presently, I realized that something terribly discordant was disrupting this natural harmony. Sounds were increasing in volume that were shattering the tranquility. Over a hill, in front of me, came some young people, seventh-graders it seemed, carrying a portable transistor radio and tape player, blasting and blaring with a kind of hard rock insanity.

It seemed to me that even the trillium withered, the hummingbird fled, and the aspen paused in their gentle quaking to shudder. Sitting down on a log as they passed, my mind began to draw pictures of a former time when Indian children of that same age would be preparing eagerly for their spiritual quest.

Having prepared for the journey with the purification of the "bath," the youth would seek out the most commanding hill for the visionary quest. There, for two nights and days, with no food or other material possessions, in prayer and meditation, the meaning and significance of the life journey ahead would be revealed and, through vision, sanctified.

The American Indians had no word in their vocabulary for either "art" or "religion." *Everything* was "art," and *everything* was "religion"; therefore, they needed no name. Everything *was sacred and related to the Great Mystery that permeates the entire creation.*

A blanket weaver is re-enacting the process of creation and a finished rug, or basket, is the image of the universe. They needed no cathedrals, no preaching, proselyting or persecution. Every moment and every act of every day was sacred, spiritual and related to the Great Mystery.

I asked myself there in that aspen glade, "What have we lost, in our obsession with something called progress?" I remembered the words of a Taos Pueblo holy man to Carl Jung: "The whites, they are always restless. We think they are mad." And Jung said, "A long series of bloodthirsty acts committed in the name of civilization crossed my mind. From our point of view we called it 'colonization,' or 'mission to the heathen,' or 'spread of civilization,' but there is the face of the predator seeking the distant quarry behind these justifications . . . ," and I asked myself again, "What have we lost?"

It has rightly been observed that if it was Indian (before the whites came), it was spiritual. The fur traders, the "Black Robe" priests, the military and then the Protestant missionaries were the men who began the disintegration of their traditions and their religion.

Today, many Native Americans are making every effort, and with a great deal of success, to once again expose their people (especially their youth) to the profound and significant traditions that are uniquely theirs.

The young people with their blaring radio, by now, had passed from sound and sight. The trillium had regained its composure, facing the life-giving energy of the sun. Hummingbirds were back riding the scented zephers; and I thought how comfortable Jesus would have been with those great spiritual people who believed everything sacred: "Consider the lilies of the field . . . look at the birds of the air . . . even Solomon in all his glory was not arrayed like one of these."

And I thought how uncomfortable Jesus would be today with the "religion" that is preached and practiced in so many of our churches and cathedrals, with its element of ostentatious display, its splendor and self-aggrandizement, its active proselytism and its open and judgmental condemnation for all other beliefs but its own.

It has been observed by many poets and seers that there is no relationship between a Jew named Jesus, walking the dusty roads of Palestine teaching some simple and beautiful insights, and the "official Christ" of the institutional church recited in dogmatic and creedal theology, built up century after century, crust over crust, into legalistic doctrines.

How ironic that it was this same theological, judgmental legalism that Jesus so scathingly attacked in the Pharisees and "church" people of his own time.

All Is Natural In The
Dance Of Existence

"Except for the still point there would be no dance . . . and there is only the dance," wrote T. S. Eliot. To live fully in joy and daily celebration, we must abandon ourselves to the dance, the dance of existence. Life is a dance and the dance goes on, with or without us.

Today, physicists are telling us that their understanding of "reality," the nature and activity of the universe, is bringing us closer and closer to the perspective of the ancient Eastern religions, especially Hinduism and classical Taoism (pronounced dow-ism).

We are a part of the cosmic dance, and all is one. Physicists assure us now that rocks and flowers dance with the dance of life. Trees dance to the wind. Salmon and trout and porpoise dance and leap with a ballet of grace and rhythm. It is asked of us even as the carpenter asked in *Alice*, "Will you, won't you, will you, won't you, will you join the dance?" Planets dance to beautifully intricate laws, even as do atoms. There is no line between the sacred and profane, the supernatural and natural, the divine and the human . . . all is natural, sacred and divine.

A recently translated Dead Sea Scroll records a disciple asking Jesus, "Master, how can we get into the Kingdom of Heaven?" Jesus answers, "Follow the birds, the beasts, the fish, and they will lead you in." Classical Taoism has been saying that for 3,000 and more years. Scholars date the origin of Taoism at least 600 years before Jesus, with the roots of this philosophy and world view going back much further.

The "Old Master" of Taoism, Lao Tzu, born about 600 B.C., was immaculately conceived by a shooting star, according to legend. Only one small volume of writings was produced by him, the Tao Te Ching, or *The Way and Its Power*. He did not preach or organize a church or any doctrine or theology. He spoke only of our at-oneness with the universe and the harmony that exists between all things. The "Tao" does not refer to a supernatural "God" . . . "out there" somewhere.

Do you want to see the living Tao? Look into a wood-burning fire and see the sun's energy dancing . . . as captured by photosynthesis. Watch a bird in flight . . . soaring on the current and never stopping to analyze or explain the wind. Listen to the sound of rain, which needs no translation. Watch a salmon leap up the next set of rapids. Watch a bee gathering honey. Watch a cucumber cucumbering.

The Tao is the way of ultimate reality. It says, "Get yourself in tune and harmony with the natural rhythms of nature and the universe, and then let yourself flow without effort, strain, tension and anxiety." It is a perspective and view of life that can be used daily in the busiest office in downtown Boise, or New York City. It changes the way you approach problems. In our busy, rushed, calendar-filled world of appointments and conferences and meetings, it can save us from migraine headaches, high blood pressure and stress problems. Whether you are a Christian, Jew, or agnostic, the beautiful themes of Taoism can still become a part of your days and activities. It can enrich your view of the world and enlarge your understanding of reality.

The flow of life is like the flow of water. If you are thrashing and flailing around, you tire and exhaust yourself and drown. If you relax and float and flow with the tide, it carries you gently. So with life. It is as Jesus said: "Consider the lilies of the field, how they grow. They neither toil nor spin. Consider the birds of the air, they neither sow nor reap. Why be anxious?"

A lovely story the Taoists tell to illustrate this attitude is of the Taoist walking along the road with a honey bucket being carried on a pole over his shoulder. The bucket slips, crashes to the ground and breaks. The Taoist continues to walk ahead, not looking back. A man seeing this event rushes up to the Taoist and yells, "Hey, your honey bucket fell, and is broken all over the ground back there." The Taoist, continuing to walk and looking straight ahead says quietly, "I know. I heard it fall," and continues without looking back. It was broken. What could he do? He could have gotten in a stew, raised his blood pressure, worried about it. But no. He quietly continued his walk.

What a difference in the living of our days, if we would remember this story at those times when the dance and the flow seem interrupted by events.

Taoists reject all forms of aggressiveness. "The axe falls first on the tallest trees," they say. "The rigid pine breaks first in the strong wind. The willow, being flexible, bends and returns its shape for another day." And again, "Nature does not have to insist. The wind can blow for only half a morning. It can rain for only half a day."

A Gnostic script presents to us a dancing Jesus at the Last Supper in the following words:

Jesus: "Those who do not dance will not comprehend what shall befall."

Disciples: "Amen."

Jesus: "Then all of you join my dance. You who dance will see what I have accomplished."

Forget The Search For Absolutes

Many of us often get locked into a dead-end canyon in our desire for absolutes. We want everything in clear cut black and white, no gray. This is truth and that is falsehood. This is good and that is bad. This is sin and that is not sin. No ifs, ands, or buts. We want all answers given clearly and simply. Unfortunately, life and reality are not that easy.

The Eastern religions ask, "How could anyone be so foolish as to think all of life and reality can be divided so easily into good and bad?"

As Pascal put it: "Truth on this side of the mountain is falsehood on the other." So what is good or what is bad depends on whether you are a Jew, Buddhist, Taoist, Druid, Christian, Hindu, Muslim or what have you.

What is good and what is bad, what is truth and what is falsehood vary day by day and situation by situation. And there are no absolutes in making decisions. Jesus not only understood this, but lived by it. Many persons bring to my attention how Jesus constantly contradicted himself, and that all of the sayings attributed to Jesus are a mass of contradictions. But I wonder if he varied his responses, his words, his actions according to the situation, in harmony with the Eastern view of these things, realizing that good and bad, right and wrong are very relative terms.

In *Matthew 10:34* Jesus says: "Do not think that I have come to bring peace on earth; I have not come to bring peace, but a sword." In another situation Jesus says in *John 14:27*, "Peace I leave with you . . . my peace I give you." In *Luke 14:28* Jesus asks: "Which of you, desiring to build a tower, does not first sit down and count the cost?" But in *Matthew 6:34*, He tells some not to worry about tomorrow and "to take no thought about what we shall eat and wear" and so forth.

In *Luke 14:26* Jesus says some unbelievable words: "If anyone comes to me and does not hate his own father and mother and wife and children and brothers and sisters, yes even his own life, he cannot be my disciple." Good heavens, what a family "breaker upper" that is. Had he not heard about the 'sacredness" of family life? And then in *John 15:12* He says, "This is my commandment, that you love one another." Of course, no one "loves" by "command." The very words are antithetical, one to the other.

How many of us are constantly looking for someone, some outside authority, to tell us how to live and what is good and what is bad? We have the feeling that somewhere is the magic well of wisdom that will give us all of the correct answers. We haunt the bookstores choosing from "self help" books by the hundreds. Or we look to some religious authority or medical authority to supply us with all of life's answers. Zen Buddhists and Taoists would only smile (or laugh) and say, "This is what is keeping you perpetually a child and crippled emotionally . . . the continuing need to have an authoritative father figure telling you the answers."

There is no master guide or key, including all of the cliches we use: Let me illustrate. We all quote glibly the Golden Rule: "Do unto others as you would have them do unto you." Nothing could be more meaningless as a blanket statement. It is a statement of reciprocity. A parent cannot always do at all what his children would wish for him to do, or what they would do in his place, or even what he would like them to do, if the roles were reversed. A question of wisdom enters and of the differences between the maturity of human beings.

Someday I am going to write a book on the thousand meaningless and absurd cliches that we all use (and some actually try to live by) daily. So recognizing that all values are relative to the mind that entertains them, and that truth "on this side of the mountain is falsehood on the other," what is our guide for making decisions in the living of these days, decisions that will enrich and free our lives, and turn every day into a joyful celebration and marvelous activity? Our guide is . . . love.

"I need to be told I AM LOVED. The realm of silence . . . is large enough beyond the grave."
                                                                    – George Eliot

"The deepest need of man (or woman) is fusion with another person in LOVE. The failure to achieve it means insanity . . . or destruction."
                                                                    – Erich Fromm

"It is impossible to find truth . . . WITHOUT BEING IN LOVE . . . for LOVE and TRUTH is the ONLY road that leads the soul out of the inner jungle."
                                                        – Abraham Joshua Heschel

"It is strange that men will talk of miracles . . . revelations . . . inspirations and the like as things past . . . while LOVE REMAINS."
                                                        – Henry David Thoreau

"Love all God's creation . . . every leaf . . . every ray of light . . . the animals . . . the plants . . . then thou wilt perceive the mystery of God."
                                                                    – Dostoevski

"Nor can anything endure which has not its foundation upon LOVE . . . for LOVE alone diminishes not."
                                                        – Queen Ludwiga of Poland
                                                          1413 A.D.

"He who does not love . . . DOES NOT KNOW GOD . . . for GOD IS LOVE. He who lives in love . . . lives in God and God lives in him."
                                                                    – I John 4:7f

THE BUFFALO SKULL AND SACRED PIPE

The buffalo to the plains Indians was the natural symbol of the universe. It was the totality of all manifestations. Eating of the shoulder meat was regarded in the same way that taking communion is regarded by the Christian. The buffalo skull was often used in sacred rituals, most notably the Sun Dance. Hanging above my stone fireplace is a magnificent skull found in a gully some miles north of Helena, Montana. The skull is rightfully facing East for to the Indian every new dawn is a sacred event.

The pipe was especially sacred and used in many different ways. Smoking the pipe is an act of communion with the forces, the Mystery, Wakan Tanka, which is behind and an integral part of the creation. It symbolized the fact that all and everything is related.

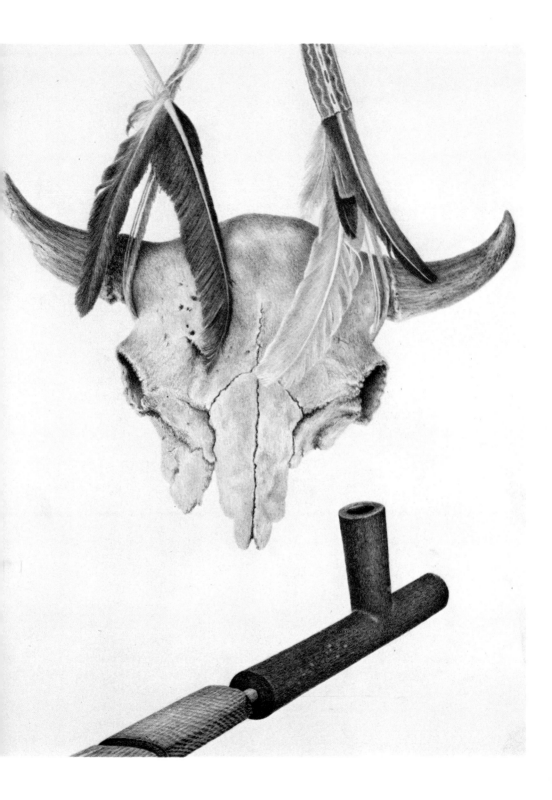

SACRED SPACE

"The defined space, the enclosure, serves as a model of the world, of the cosmos, or microcosmically of the beings of nature. Essential to such a definition of space is the ritualized means by which to fix the centers of sacredness. A ritually defined center is taken to be the actual center of the world."
— *Jamake Highwater*
The Primal Mind

"The first function of myths and mythic rituals . . . sacred songs and ceremonial dances . . . is TO WAKEN IN THE INDIVIDUAL A SENSE OF AWE . . . WONDER . . . AND PARTICIPATION IN THE MYSTERY OF BEING."
— *Joseph Campbell*

"For the understanding of religions . . . a complete understanding of myth is mandatory."
— *Mircea Eliade*

"It is the object of myth to explain the world . . . as in 'Once Upon a Time'."
— *Pierre Grimal*
Professor at the Sorbonne

"Living myths do not come out of books."
— *Joseph Campbell*

Religion's Roots Reflect The Landscape

One of the most fascinating subjects in the study of religions is the influence of the landscape on the formation of religious doctrines and concepts.

The pantheon of any particular group is usually directly related to the type of land and landscape they live with. An agricultural society has gods and goddesses for sun, rain, storms and the like, and above all for fertility. A rich, lush land gives rise to nymphs, satyrs and spirits of woods and water. The Northwest Indian lived in giant rain forests, dark, dreary and forboding. Their world of spirits and religious mythology was all directly related to that landscape.

Gatherers of nuts, seeds and roots, living hand to mouth on more barren landscapes, developed religious concepts and myths that were in harmony with their type of existence. To those whose landscape was the Southwest, a Papago said it best: "We desert people have no rivers. All our water is in the sky."

Taoism harmonizes beautifully with the landscape of much of China with mountains and mist, waterfalls and rich vegetation. The austere God of Judaism, Islam and Christianity came from the austerity of a bleak desert. A Moslem mosque is a stylized oasis.

People who live in mountains see things differently from those living on the vast, spaceless dimensions of the plains or the desert. How well I remember, when I was a Marine Corps pilot, control tower personnel in the desert giving me visibility of 100 miles, compared to the four and five miles of more humid areas. These are different worlds.

There were different landscapes with different conditions for the Neanderthal theologian, Buddhist theologian, Hebrew theologian and Greek theologian. Greek temples were built on hills overlooking the Mediterranean. The Greeks had a sense of nature, and the temples blended beautifully into the landscape.

From the landscape, religions come into being. To the Hebrews of the Old Testament, the austere desert spoke of an austere, stern God. And if you are a people wandering over it for 40 years, the God who put you there must be as stern as the land itself to inflict such upon you. And you dream; you dream of a paradise of lush gardens where there will be milk and honey, vineyards and fruit trees. There you will create a God of love, for religions of love are religions of the well-fed.

How well the late General Douglas MacArthur realized this. In his famous address to the joint session of Congress upon his return from Korea he said: "You cannot talk to people about idealistic philosophical concepts or principles until first you put food in their stomachs, clothing on their backs and a roof over their head." Religions of love are religions of the well-fed. When the crops are in and the stomach is full,

25

there is time to rest and meditate under the shade of an olive tree. Then you can think of brotherhood.

It is interesting that the first Old Testament writer to present God as a God of love is Hosea, a man who was ardently in love with the land. He wrote of domestic animals, agricultural life, of fruits, flowers and the thistles of the field, of winds and rains.

The landscape even continues to influence our religious orientation and responses. It is no accident that the lowest church attendance in the U.S. is in the Pacific Northwest and Colorado. Why? The beauty of the landscape calls us, the majestic mountains, rushing rivers and sparkling lakes surrounded by blankets of alpine flowers. How often I have heard, "I feel closer to God out there in the mountains than I do in any church building." In this magnificent country I can understand why. When Winston Churchill stood on the south rim of the Grand Canyon of Arizona for the first time, he said it was such an awesome spiritual experience that he wanted to fall to his knees. A sand field of west Texas or corn stubble in Oklahoma would probably not have evoked such a spiritual response. I know, having grown up in Texas and Oklahoma. On Sunday mornings there just was not much else to do but go to church.

What I am saying is that from the land and landscapes, religions and gods are born and later on transformed to be in harmony with the existing land and landscape of any given region.

The God of Judaism, Christianity and Islam had its origin in a desert.

The poet Walt Kaufmann wrote, "Desert born God, sandstorm cradled; time is burning blistering justice, fiery darkness that blinds and destroys. Trees that are kissing sand whirling ground, loving the storm that snaps their trunks: I shall not bow to merciless glory. Thine is the desert in which you are buried; thine is the darkness that was your mother . . . desert born God, sandstorm cradled."

Buildings, Art Can Act
As Enriching Shrines

Since I have spent this past year avoiding controversial issues in my columns, and have dealt with such safe subjects as Billy Graham, the 10 Commandments, euthanasia and Biblical mythology, I thought it time to gather up my courage and dive into a controversial issue and take a stand. The time has come to address the Boise downtown debate and the relationship of public art to the city. You may be asking, what has that got to do with "religion"? The answer is everything.

The earliest cities began as tribal shrine centers. A perfect example is the city of Catal Huyuk, going back to 6000 B.C., in south central Turkey. The city, the shrines and its art were inseparable and perceived as one. Shrine centers were located at what was believed to be the axis of the universe, the one place where the earth and the gods connected. Murals were painted freehand on walls by artists. The colors were strong and vivid. Every third building in the downtown was a shrine where the most elaborate art work has been found, with religious overtones. Cities were "holy" in the truest sense of the word, and magnificent art contributed to that "holiness" or the "whole-ness" of both the city and the people. Cities were and are places where human beings confront the implications of their "humanity" and what it means to be truly "human." A sense of holiness increased through use.

There is an Arabic word, "Baraka," which means the blessedness that attaches itself to buildings or objects after years of loving use. During World War II, the chambers of the House of Commons in England were blown up. Winston Churchill urged that they be rebuilt exactly as they once were. In a spirited speech, he emphasized that changing the architecture would affect the manner of debates and, as a result, the structure of English democracy. He dramatized the interplay between human beings and their buildings.

Centers of buildings and objects, symbols of years of loving use, are being fragmented today and pulled apart by three technological trends: First, increased transportation systems; Second, electrical energy available outside the cities; and Third, improved communications networks, all of which stimulate the growth of satellite shopping malls. But a price must be paid for the scattering and fragmentation of our communal life and that price is a loss of communal identification, pride, orientation, and perhaps most important of all, cultural enrichment.

A major factor in pulling the downtown area of a city together with a renewed sense of identification and enrichment is public art. There is a sense in which all great art is religious. The Renaissance at its best took seriously the sacredness of the human being and the contribution of great art, music and literature (the humanities) to human and cultural enrichment. The value of public art is that it provides a central expression and focus. It can become the symbol and the trademark, even the logo, of a community.

The most perfect example is that of a Midwest, conservative city, Grand Rapids, Michigan. In the mid 1960s, a committee composed of local citizens considered 10 artists for a sculpture in the downtown City Hall plaza. Alexander Calder, the preeminent American sculptor of the 20th century, was chosen to do the work. The title would be La Grande Vitesse (the "great swiftness") or "The Grand Rapids." It would be 55 feet long, 43 feet high and weigh 42 tons. It was dedicated June 14, 1969, and has become the uniquely identifiable symbol of that city. It is the largest Calder stabile in the Western Hemisphere. Today, even the sanitation trucks of Grand Rapids carry the symbol of La Grande Vitesse. But in the beginning . . . let me tell you of "in the beginning."

When the committee first announced what it was planning with Calder, it was crucified by local citizens. Members of the committee received threats on their lives from anonymous telephone callers and letter writers. Yes, the chairwoman actually received threats on her life if she did not cancel the project.

But they endured and they proceeded. Today, the Calder La Grande Vitesse is pictured and mentioned always in the same breath with Grand Rapids, Mich. When *The New York Times Magazine* ran a feature on Grand Rapids (after Gerald Ford became President) they chose for the cover a brilliant color picture of the red Calder sculpture. A city which was incorporated in 1850 is now symbolized all over the world, 133 years later, by a piece of modern sculpture. And, please do not miss this point . . . that to start the Calder sculpture, the city officials approved an expense of $7,000 to tear up and remove plumbing that had already been installed by those who wanted a fountain placed on the spot.

What has happened since the Calder was completed? On the same plaza, the community has a large metal sculpture by Nate Horowitz, a previously unrecognized local sculptor. The flat roof of the county Administration Building adjacent to City Hall and the Calder stabile has been painted with a Calder design commissioned for that space, which is 127 feet square, making it the largest Calder painting in the world, and the only rooftop to be so decorated. Stairwells and the lobby of the city-county buildings have been painted with supergraphics designed and executed by local artists. And a recent monumental earth sculpture was completed by the major American artist, Robert Morris. A contemporary work of art has recently been placed on top of the salmon fish ladder in the Grand River. The Calder sculpture also became the backdrop of an annual three-day arts festival that draws more than 300,000 persons.

The Calder work set off an artistic explosion that makes the downtown area of Grand Rapids known all over the United States (and the world) as a symbol of city and community vision and pride. Public art is a community symbol. Grand Rapids wanted its symbol to be the finest execution of excellence that money could buy. His work became a major force in the creation of a sense of community.

All great art is religious and reflects the values of humankind. It need not be, and should not be, confined to the inside of museums and churches. When placed outside on the plazas and sidewalks of cities it can become a source of pride and identification.

Euripides advised his Hellenic audience: "The first requisite for happiness is that a person be born in a great city." Boise can become such a city.

FANATICS, ROAD SHOWS
AND MATURE RELIGION

"50,000 people in the Dallas Cotton Bowl . . . screaming at the top of their lungs . . . 'Jesus . . . Jesus . . . Jesus' . . . IT WAS CHAOS . . ."
                                   – Vine Deloria

"The traditions of our orthodox Christian culture give powerful support and impetus to cultic fantasies and fanaticism."
                                   – Weston LaBarre, Ph.D., Chairman
                                   Department of Anthropology, Duke
                                   University

"The majority of the cults claim links to Christianity."
                                   – Dr. Walter Martin
                                   cultic movements scholar

Religious Fanatics Use "Truth"
To Justify Violence

We have all been shocked at the assassination of Anwar Sadat by religious fanatics. What ideas inflame such religious fanaticism? Where do they find their justification for such violence?

The historian Arnold Toynbee said that before you can understand any culture or any people, you first must understand their religion. A recent editorial in the *Wall Street Journal* confirmed the same observation in these words: "The study of religion is so vitally important in today's world that it should be mandatory at the university level of education. No one should graduate without having studied comparative world religions."

Religious concepts that dominate Islam and Christianity (and to a far lesser degree, Judaism) have their origin in Zoroastrianism. The religious historian and scholar, Walter Kaufmann, puts it in these words in his book, *Religion in Four Dimensions:* "The Christianity of St. Augustine, the material of the four gospels and the letters of St. Paul are all saturated with Zoroastrianism."

Joseph Campbell adds this thought: "The dialogue between the Persian God Mazda and his chosen divine son, Zoroaster, can be heard echoed and re-echoed in Greek, Hebrew, Arabic, Christianity and every tongue of the West."

Who was Zoroaster? He was born around 800 to 900 B.C. We are talking about legends that were prevalent in Persia 900 years before Jesus. His conception was divine, born of a virgin. A ray of heaven's glory entered the bosom of a maid of noble lineage. On the day of his birth all of the evil spirits fled in terror.

He was a lover of righteousness who withdrew into the desert. There the Devil tempted him, but to no avail. He resisted Satan (a Zoroastrian concept) and clung to his faith in Mazda, the supreme Lord of Light, God. God gave to him the Avesta, the book of knowledge and wisdom and told him to preach it to all mankind. He was ridiculed, persecuted and died. Upon his death, he ascended into heaven.

In Zoroastrianism is the belief that human beings have free will and are not pawns in a cosmic war. Human beings are free to make a choice, to throw their weight on one side or the other, darkness and evil, or light and goodness.

Zoroaster believed the earth could be reformed by human action. Virtue lay in engagement. It is the duty of human beings to stamp out evil. It is a cosmic principle. There is evil and there is good. Evil will be stamped out only when enough human beings make the choice to choose good.

Satan, the Devil, The Prince of Darkness, all had their origin in Zoroastrianism. For those who choose evil, there will be the Last Judgment (again, a concept whose origin is Zoroastrian) complete with hell and purgatory. Islam and Christianity borrowed heavily from these Zoroastrian ideas.

This leads us into the dimensions of religious violence and fanaticism. If the earth is a battleground between good and evil, with the good being rewarded in a "paradise" (a Persian concept) called "heaven" and the bad being punished by a Last Judgment in a place called "hell," it is a very short jump to imagine that you represent "good" and all others are "bad."

And if it is a battle between the good guys and the bad guys, it is also a very short jump to justify anything you do to the bad guys. You, being a good guy, are making this earth a place where your brand of justice, righteousness and goodness shall prevail. With heaven as a reward, there is even the added motivation to clean up the bad.

When the degree of psychotic religious fanaticism is reached that you are one of the few who know "truth," and all others are "infidels" and "heretics," then every form of murder and violence can be justified on religious grounds. The Islamic fanatics and assassins refer to it as a "sacred hatred," the sending of "infidels" on the hell they deserve, while on their part anticipating their glorious rewards in heaven.

"The True Believer," Eric Hoffer writes, "is responsible for the majority of all the human suffering on this planet." The "true believer" stands as the primary obstacle in building a planet of brotherhood where "not even a sparrow falls to the ground unknown . . . and the least shall be considered side by side with the greatest."

Religious Right Threatens Our Right To A Free Mind

As the 4th of July approaches with all that magnificent day is symbolic of, there are words and names that play upon my mind. Consider the brilliance and genius of our Founding Fathers. Will we ever again see their stature? I often wonder, and prayerfully hope.

Thomas Jefferson: "I have sworn upon the altar of God eternal hostility against every form of tyranny over the mind of man." (Political and religious.)

Thomas Paine: "Those who expect to reap the blessings of freedom must, like men undergo the fatigue of supporting it."

Benjamin Franklin: "Those who would give up essential freedoms to purchase a little temporary safety . . . deserve neither liberty or safety."

The glory of it. It makes your blood run faster. It makes you shiver with admiration.

We live daily, in every area of our lives, on the interest of the principle that has been paid. Liberty . . . Freedom . . . "We hold these truths to be self-evident."

We have struggled against dictators, tyrants, bigots, dogmatists, against forces of slavery and evil, against those who would shackle and close the mind to free thought and expression. But we have endured. And it has cost much pain and much blood.

America has been the symbol of the free mind. A Frenchman gave us a statue for a great new free nation, and a Jewish girl wrote the words for it: "Give me your tired, your poor, your huddled masses yearning to breathe free."

This is America. And yet we have seen group after group make an attempt to kill this thing that is America. First it was the Klan which was going to scare people into "pure" Americanism. We endured the McCarthy era and the crucifixion of good people in the name of "pure" Americanism.

Do we have so little faith in our own philosophy that we cannot expose it to the open market of free ideas? Can we no longer debate contradicting ideas and philosophies on their merits without resorting to tactics that we despised in Hitler and Stalin?

Some people don't like evolution; some don't like labor unions, civil rights or the NAACP. Some don't like different colored human beings or any religious ideas that differ from their own. Some don't like liberals or conservatives or any social or economic ideas that seem strange. And any idea that differs is the start of something evil, so they say.

They don't want any ideas taught that are alien to them, and so they attempt to tell the church and the schools what they can teach, what books they can read, what movies they can see, what ideas can be explored, and where does it end? Can you imagine, in America? "America" should mean that no group can assume the right to tell other people what they must believe, how they must act, what books are "safe," and what opinions are "approved."

"History tells me that persecution comes from people who want to make others good," wrote Roland Hegstad, editor of the *Seventh Day Adventist* magazine. And he continued, "How ironic, to lose our freedom at last, not to leftists tossing bombs, but to Christians espousing slogans and cliches."

The academic dean of Stanford University recently wrote this in their *University* magazine: "The Christian Right and the Moral Majority are potentially much more dangerous to our nation than the Communist Party ever has been. This group presents the gravest crisis of this century in the next two decades, because of their wedding of religious "slogans" with their politics. They are infringing upon a precious right, that each of us inherited from those learned men of the 18th century who expressly separated church and state in these United States of America."

United States Supreme Court Justice Potter Stewart was known on the high court as a moderate and a conservative. He, in an interview with the *Christian Science Monitor,* expressed his grave concern over the threat to the Constitution. And in an editorial in that same newspaper were these words: "Today our Constitution is under a severe challenge . . . which should stir every American."

Bishop James Armstrong of the Methodist Church and the president of the National Council said it in this manner, "The unbelievable arrogance (of the Christian Right), the arrogance that says 'if you do not agree with me, you are neither a patriot or a Christian'."

On September 17, 1787, the Constitution of the United States guaranteed us our freedoms, if we, as a free people, assume responsibility for them. Behind a thick glass at the National Archives are four sheets of parchment, written in longhand with indigo ink. This document is the heart of representative democracy and due process of law.

On the 4th of July weekend, will you remember with me some words written by the poet Stephen Vincent Benet. Remember them, memorize them, read them to your children, your neighbors and friends. And read them again and again.

"There are certain words
Our own and others we're used to . . . words we've used,
Heard, had to recite. Forgotten,
Rubbed shiny in the pocket, left home for keepsakes,
Inherited, stuck away in the back drawer,

In the locked trunk, at the back of the quiet mind
Liberty . . . equality . . . freedom
To none will we sell, refuse or deny, right or justice,
We hold these truths to be self-evident.
I am merely saying . . . what if these words pass?
What if they pass and are gone and are no more?
It took long to buy these words.
It took a long time to buy them . . . and much pain."

"Freedom . . . the absence of coercion or constraint in choice or action . . .
liberation from the power of another . . . liberation from restraint"
– Webster's Dictionary

"Heresy . . . from the Greek 'hairesis' . . . meaning 'freedom to
CHOOSE'."
– Webster's Dictionary

"Our symbol of faith is heresy. Tomorrow is inevitably heresy to today. We
march in the name of TOMORROW'S FREE MAN."
– Yevgeny Zamyatin (1884-1937)

"Heresy is being right when the 'right' thing to do is to continue being
wrong."
– Anon

"The price of freedom and liberty is the loss of the love of paternalistic
authority."

Mr. TV Evangelist, When Do You Do Unglamorous Preacher Work?

An open letter to a Hollywood, Glamorous, "Whole Gospel," Moral Majority, Television Evangelist:

Dear Mr. Television Evangelist:

Lately now I have been wondering about you, especially since you are getting so big in these United States with such a following and raking in so much money. Last year evangelists like you bought more than $600 million worth of television time alone.

Well now, if you pay $600 million, what must you be taking in? It causes me a great deal of suspicious concern that one of you projects a take of *2 billion* in the next five years. You will generate a cash flow of more than $750 million this year alone. By comparison, the combined budget of the United Presbyterian Church in the U.S.A. and the United Church of Christ comes to only $45 million.

But there is more than that, Mr. Star Personality . . . *more than money.* I like what an editor of the *Saturday Review* said, that your "message is nothing but pure emotional fervor, a video-induced adrenalin for the childish religious nervous systems, offering nothing but the most simple answers for difficult and complex questions, answers so absurd as to stagger the enlightened mind."

I have not agreed with Barry Goldwater on some things, but I loved him when he said this to you in national publications: "I am warning you . . . I will fight you every step of the way when you try to dictate your moral convictions to all Americans under the name of conservatism. I am sick and tired of you political preachers on television telling me that if I am to be a 'moral' person, I must believe in A, B, C or D . . . just who do you think you are?"

Another thing, Mr. Evangelist, you remain in your plush television studios, raking in millions, and are not responsible for meeting any of the genuine, authentic needs of any Christian church community in this nation. You do not have to plan the hayrides and skating parties for our young people, and round up chaperones, and spend time in their nurture . . . the nurture that counts.

You never have to sit into the late hours of a night and cry with Mr. Jones while his wife is dying of cancer. You never have to take phone calls at one a.m. that wake you out of a sound sleep, calls by someone who says, "I'm sorry, I know it's late, but I just wanted someone to talk to." You never have to spend days visiting with a bereaved family over funeral arrangements and hold their hands, crying with them as they recall happy hours from the past. You never have to stand by a grave month after month, year after year; and each time gaze with moist eyes at the family in the folding chairs under the awning and wonder, "What can I say that will help this family?"

You never have to do any one of these unglamorous things for which there are no spotlights, no 2,000-voice choir, no 2,000 blooming chrysanthemums, no orchestra, no big showbiz names, no Johnny Cash. Where very few even know about what you do, you talk about preaching the whole gospel — what a tragic farce!

What about Mrs. John Doe in East Bend, Idaho, who has been sending you hundreds of dollars because you are so wonderful with your whole gospel? When she dies, are you going to come out and bury her in your $500 suit and your $150 pair of shoes and cry with her husband? No, you will not be here. Who will be here burying her? Some unglamorous preacher in a frayed suit, in scuffed shoes, who has not seen in his lifetime what you make in five minutes of air time.

Well, Mr. Hollywood, Glamorous Television Preacher Evangelist, I have only a few last questions for you and your staff with your limousines and your plush living, you who claim to present the WHOLE GOSPEL of Jesus Christ.

When is the last time that you spent an hour in the hot sun with a woman at the well, distressed over her condition and offered her genuine, lasting, living water?

You who preach the *whole gospel*, when is the last time you came on the air and said quite simply, "All of you who love are not far from the kingdom of God," and then signed off. When, Mr. Preacher?

I remind you, there was one, once, who told an inquirer in clear words of what the whole gospel consisted. A scribe said to Jesus of Nazareth, "I love God . . . with my mind and my heart . . . and my neighbor as myself . . ." And to this scribe, Jesus replied, "You are very close to the Kingdom . . ."

That is the WHOLE GOSPEL Mr. Hollywood Glamorous Television Star, AND IT IS ALL FREE.

Truly Spiritual People Don't Need Evangelistic Hoopla

The Billy Graham road show has come and gone.

Once again, as in three other cities where I have lived, Boise has returned to normal.

The bars are still full at the 5 o'clock happy hour, with some happy and some lonely people; church attendance is just about what it has always been.

Twelve-voice choirs are again struggling with next Sunday's anthem, their members thinking nostalgically of a short week ago when they hit big-time show biz in a 1,500-voice choir, all in pastels, humming *Just As I Am* in front of 500 carnation plants and rubbing elbows with musical celebrities of national prominence.

Ministerial dignitaries, who were invited to sit on the platform with Billy, are now back behind their desks trying to figure out how to meet their budgets and increase their memberships. I have never understood how some of those clergy sitting on the platform could have so swallowed their integrity by accepting the invitation, considering that their knowledge, theology and "beliefs" are far more enlightened than what Billy was preaching. Maybe it is as a bishop friend in Oklahoma City said, "Just good church politics to be seen up there. It is good exposure."

I have never understood how Billy and his staff can keep telling people what the "Holy Spirit" is doing for them, and that it is the "Holy Spirit" who fills the arena. Consider the fact that all seats are free and that the crusade staff has been working for one year to prepare the city with an efficiency and a fervor that would make "Madison Avenue public relations people look like beginners" (in the words of one man involved). I watched them working in both Oklahoma City (where I was involved) and Seattle.

In Boise, according to figures reported in *The Idaho Statesman*, between 5,000 and 10,000 people have been working contacting 78,000 homes, with massive sell that is without precedent for Pavilion shows. This is in addition to 100 billboards and full-page advertisements in the newspaper, plus continual television advertisements. What all of this says is that the Holy Spirit needs lots and lots of help to fill that arena. How interesting it would be to see what the Holy Spirit could do by herself.

By comparison, the Beach Boys drew 11,000 and, rather than giving seats away, they charged $12.50 a person. They came in with practically no advance publicity (compared to Billy) and they did not even offer salvation as a bonus. How refreshing that not once did the Beach Boys claim that the Holy Spirit had filled their arena.

My thoughts return to the Oklahoma City crusade and to the invitation that Billy gave at the end of his speech. It was a speech full of fear and judgment and what God (who had a computer no doubt) was going to do to all of us sinners who did not pay attention to what Billy was telling us.

The time came for the invitation. There was a full moon, 500 chrysanthemum plants on the stage, a 3,000-voice choir humming *Just As I Am*. The outdoor arena lights were turned down. The setting was breathtaking in its emotional manipulation — so breathtaking, in fact, that a person could have been reading the laundry list from the pulpit and all of us would have been crying for joy. I cannot remember if the choir was all in pastels as in Boise, but it would have made no difference. They could have been in overalls.

In your quiet moments of solitude and reverence, you might ask, "What would Jesus really think of all of that Hollywood hyperbole?" There is something missing. It seems to me to be a true spirituality.

Spiritually centered people and leaders do not need gimmicks. Truly great saints come to my mind: Francis of Assisi, Meister Eckhart, Thomas Merton, Albert Schweitzer, Dag Hammarskjold . . .

Where would it end, the list of saints and spirits who have made their quiet, profound testimony in the spirit of the One of Nazareth who met the woman at the well and sat on the porch of Mary and Martha, without choirs, carnations, television cameras and all of the rest of the hoopla that goes with evangelistic ego trips?

Perhaps the ultimate ego trip is to stand in front of people and tell them that "Unless you listen to me and my message . . . and unless you believe what I am telling you about God . . . you are doomed . . . you have had it on God's computer." This must be the ultimate in spiritual blackmail. In a universe of a hundred million galaxies, beyond all human comprehension, a man stands up in a little spot on a little speck of the cosmic beach called Earth and tells you what the Mystery behind all of this is going to do to you if you do not listen to him.

Billy and his show have gone. In the spirit of Jesus, our brother of Nazareth, pastors and laity again are going quietly about their business, making their quiet testimony with sweat and tears and joy . . . and marrying people and burying people . . . and on Sunday, still, in the words of the poet Alan Paton,

"hearing some organ play and hearing some people sing . . .

and hearing about some money that is needed . . .

and some message given by some man or woman, sometimes with distinction, and sometimes with none . . .

Sometimes seeing Him not, and sometimes clearly with inward eye . . .

And saying in our heart to Him . . .

Reach out Thy hands and touch me most Holy One."

Heretics Often Light Way Toward Truth — And God

Regardless of what vocation you are in, it is very easy to tell if you are a heretic. How can you tell? Someone, friend (so called) or colleague, will confront you with "do you mean that you DO NOT BELIEVE THAT . . . ?"

How endless are the things you might not believe that you are *supposed* to believe. If you are in the church, you might be confronted with "Do you mean that you do not believe that the world has been saved by Jesus Christ shedding his blood on the cross for you?"

The attitude is, not believing in that is like not believing in the gall bladder or the Seattle Seahawks.

A Taoist cares nothing about what you "believe" about Jesus, or a Hindu or a Jew. What is "heresy" for one person will be considered totally irrelevant by another person and a magnificent stand for free thought by a third person. All values are relative to the mind that entertains them.

The brilliant federal judge, Learned Hand, used these words in praising heresy: "The organization or society that has smothered heretics has always declined."

The word "heresy" originally had a very positive meaning. It comes from a Greek verb meaning "to choose." It means a personal choice. But where there is no freedom, there can be no free choice because free choices are not welcome and are threatening to authoritative voices. Heresy is, in reality, nothing more than making a choice against the accepted belief of the majority.

Heretics are a catalyst in society. They are a mutative factor, creating change with new thoughts, concepts and ideas that point in a new direction.

Jesus Christ was a great heretic. The people cried heresy after He spoke and taught. Christianity is a heresy of Judaism. Buddhism is a heresy of Hinduism. Christianity was bursting with heresies in its youthful growth.

America was settled by pilgrims who were heretics. The pioneers who settled the Western United States were heretics.

Think of the heretics of civilization who have contributed to our growth and enlightenment, such as Freud, Einstein, Darwin — and where would the list end?

The church "fathers" believed that the sun moved around the earth and that the earth was the center of the universe. Thank God for the heretics, Copernicus and Galileo, who revealed the truth to the church that it was just the opposite — that the earth moved around the

40

sun and was not only not the center of the universe, but was not even a major part of our own little galaxy.

If God is "truth," as Jesus and others have said, then wherever "truth" is, God is. And far more often than not, it has been the heretics who have pointed us toward truth, toward God, while the authoritative, dogmatic institutions tremble, defending their archaic cosmologies and mythologies.

There is a continuing, mandatory need for heresy in its most profound sense; for freedom to choose and to follow "truth," wherever it leads. The essence of the faith of a free people is freedom of choice, which is the definition of heresy.

Religiously Educated — What Does It Mean?

The late Robert Hutchins was dean of Yale University Law School at age 28. He was appointed chancellor of the University of Chicago at age 32. He was obviously brilliant.

One of the most important events of his life, and one he never forgot, took place when he was a teenager.

His father was professor of theology at Oberlin College in Ohio. Robert Hutchins went to his father one day and began to give him his opinion about a particular subject, when his father stopped him with these words: "Son, let me remind you before you proceed, that you do not know enough about the subject to even have an opinion."

Would to God that every Tom, Jane, Dick and Harry going around giving their "opinions" about religion and the Bible would take that to heart. As Dr. Fred Denbeaux put it in the Layman's Theological Library series: "The person who is unwilling to study linguistics and literary distinctions and to differentiate between prose and poetry, history and mythology, legend and folklore, will not ever understand the Bible."

If the Bible is such an easy to understand book, why is it that we have over 700 different, fragmented Protestant denominations all reading the Bible differently? Add to this the Roman Catholics, Jews and Eastern Orthodox with other interpretations, as well as literary scholars with yet other views of the material. Add to this the fact, as reported in many national publications, that within even one single body of Protestantism — the Lutherans — there are continual internal fights as to how to "read" the Bible. The battles are to such an extent that almost an entire theological seminary faculty was fired.

There is an enormous amount of confusion as to what it means to be religiously educated. There is a vast difference between education, indoctrination and training.

Let me illustrate: I had an acquaintance at Oklahoma State University who had a Ph.D. degree in poultry science. (And I do wish they would stop calling those Ph.D. degrees "doctor of philosophy." He was not a philosophy major. He was a doctor of poultry science.) He knew all there was to know, at that time, about chickens, I am sure of that. But, outside of chickens, he was one of the most uninformed, poorly read, unlettered men I have ever known. A "functional illiterate" as they say. And his "opinions" on religion, Christianity and the Bible were about as enlightened and informed as those of my dog.

And yet people assumed that because he had his Ph.D. he was "educated" when nothing could have been further from the truth. He was a "trained" technician or "specialist" in poultry science and nothing more.

A dentist friend of mine in Tacoma, Washington, was teaching Bible classes. He was so religiously illiterate that when I told him the *Old Testament* was an English translation of Hebrew, he was amazed. And he often told me that he refused to believe that Jesus was a Jew. And he was teaching Bible classes. Even worse, people were listening to him. They assumed that because he had a degree in dentistry that he was "educated" and could teach the Bible. The blind leading the blind would be an understatement.

How swayed and duped we are by titles and by so called credentials that may not be either accurate or legitimate. (As a side note on the doctor of divinity title used by so many ministers: In the vast majority of cases it is not an earned degree at all but an honorary one given by a church-related college of the minister's own denomination. It is not an academically earned degree obtained through study.)

I am asking the question: What does it mean to be religiously educated?

Anthropologists estimate that over the past 150,000 years there have been at least 100,000 distinctly different religions. How can anyone preach, teach, speak, lecture intelligently about the Bible or Christianity, if he/she has no idea where they fit into that 150,000 year religious jigsaw puzzle?

The vast majority within the Christian church have been exposed to, trained in and indoctrinated with only one religion, which leaves about 99,999 others. And out of 150,000 years have been exposed to only a very brief 2,000-year period, which leaves the other 148,000 years out, like they were of no importance to the last 2,000. You might call this a very minute, exceedingly restrictive and narrow understanding of religion, the Bible and Christianity.

There is nothing in this column to invalidate personal, private spiritual experiences. That is a totally different matter from giving uninformed and ignorant opinions about the Bible and religion.

What does it mean to be religiously educated? It means to have seriously exposed yourself to primitive religions (the Bible is loaded with primitive religion), comparative religions, comparative mythologies, the origins of religions and religious literature, semantics, linguistics and symbolism, the history of religions and related disciplines — either formally in a university or seriously in your own private studies and readings.

It is not easy to read intelligently and to think precisely; it is not easy to speak fluently and write clearly; it is not easy to study a subject carefully and know it thoroughly. But these abilities are the foundation of a sound education, including a religious and Christian education. Becoming a religiously educated person is a difficult, demanding enterprise. But, if it is all as important as we claim it to be, then surely it is worth the effort.

Mature Religion Taps Divine Potential

Men and women fight over religion. Certainly it is not mature expressions of religious dimensions they fight over or they could not be fighting.

In the name of "religion" we fight "holy" wars, enter upon bloody crusades, and foment hate. The language of religion even evokes terror in many, as today in Belfast, Beirut, Israel, "Christian" militiamen, Palestine, Moslem civilians, Lebanon, Iran, Islamic fundamentalists — and where does it end?

A requisite of religious maturity is the ability to evaluate what we mean by the language we use, without prejudice and without allowing them to impede our quest for truth.

What do we mean by "religion?" And what is mature religion?

The inquisitor of Lorraine caused nearly 900 witches and sorcerers to be burned to death within 15 years (1575-1590). On his death bed he said that he had a terrible feeling of guilt. Why guilt? Because he had spared a few children and not killed them. "Is it right to spare baby vipers . . . baby witches?" he asked. For this man, that was religion.

The Crusades . . . were they expressions of mature religion? The Inquisition . . . was that religion? Belfast today . . . is that mature religion?

The most horrible blasphemy against God, mature religion, and all that is holy . . . is not questioning some belief or some institution. The most horrible blasphemy is the perversion and the denial of love, mercy and human sanctification. And this, too, even includes religion as revealed in the Bible. When Moses gave commands to destroy women and children of enemy tribes, he claimed it was in the name of God, and God commanded it. What blasphemy against all that is holy and all that is decent! In the name of religion, men and women have sanctioned every cruelty, prejudice, witchcraft, ignorance, supersition, sorcery, poverty and injustices.

What is mature religion. Is it the fetish worship of an aborigine? The rantings of an evangelist? Is it a Buddhist monk singing praises or a Unitarian lecture?

We apply the term religion to Taoists, Buddhists, Druids, Shakers, Calvinists, Hottentots, Southern Baptists, and the snake handlers of Tennessee and Arkansas. We apply the word to Jehovah's Witnesses, Christian Scientists, and Presbyterians, to Jews, Pantheists, and Pentecostals.

There is a vast difference between primitive, crude, immature, and even pathological low versions of something called religion and between mature, elevated, prophetic, high and creative religion.

What is mature religion? Mature religion has at its base freedom, enlightenment, compassion, love and mercy. Its ritual is for one purpose only — to awaken people to their divine potential for holiness (whole-ness), beauty, truth and justice. Mature religion is dedicated to the elevation of humans rather than the elevation of the institutions.

Abraham Lincoln belonged to no church; refused to be baptized or take communion; confirmed no doctrines and was never identified with institutional religion; and yet, a more deeply religious man has never occupied the White House.

The Harvard psychologist, Gordon Allport, defined mature and immature, childish religion. I like his definitions:

Immature and childish religion is rigid and compulsive dogmatism; it's holier-than-thou intolerance, an insatiable need for crutches and reassurance; obsessive ritualism; fear of sins and a regressive dependence. By contrast, he defines mature religion this way:

• The maturely religious person is self-critical and has insights into himself. He is not insecure nor threatened. He can question and doubt; he can analyze and evaluate his beliefs.

• Mature religion has a motivational force of its own . . . and needs no outside authority.

• Mature religion inspires, influences and motivates the behavior of the individual.

• Mature religion sees the relationship of experience to God . . . and looks upon life as an integrated pattern.

The criterion of mature religion is the dynamism that makes a person a persistent searcher after light and truth with the recognition that the quest is a continuous and eternal one. Mature religion understands too, that faith is not belief; but rather, faith is resting comfortably and securely in the knowledge that we are part of a divine plan.

TAI CHI DISK

The Tai Chi disk is the symbol for yin and yang. The entire cosmos, including you and me, is composed of complimentary opposites, never static, rigid or frozen but constantly evolving. If you could be above a mountain and spend the day watching the light and shadows moving and changing positions you would see yin and yang. 'Yang' is the sunny side of the mountain and 'yin' the shady side. Heaven is yang and the earth is yin. Male is yang and female is yin. There is light and darkness, negative and positive, spring and fall, summer and winter, and all of the complimentary opposites that make up the 'nature' of the universe. No other religious or philosophical symbol so completely expresses the flowing and unfolding nature of truth. All of the great religious traditions from Christianity to Buddhism, Taoism to the American Indian, Hinduism to Islam find accommodation within this symbol.

FAITH IS NOT BELIEF

"Faith is NOT belief . . . and it is NOT knowledge with a low degree of probability."
                                                                    – Paul Tillich

"There is love and faith without the acceptance of any beliefs or doctrine. History has shown that the most terrible crimes against love have been committed in the name of fanatically defended beliefs and doctrines."
                                                                    – Ibid

"The deepest truth that I have discovered is that if one accepts the loss of 'beliefs' . . . if one gives up clinging to what is irretrievably gone . . . then the nothing which is left is not barren . . . but enormously fruitful.
                                                                    – Robert Bellah

God, to me, it seems is a verb
       not a noun, proper or improper . . .
God is the articulation, not the art,
       objective or subjective;
God is loving, not the abstraction 'love'
       commanded or entreated;
God is knowledge dynamic, not legislative
       code, not proclamation law, not academic
       dogma, not ecclesiastic canon.

Yes, God is a verb, the most active . . ."
       – excerpts from "No More Secondhand God"
                                                                    – Buckminster Fuller

Genuine Faith Surpasses Mere Beliefs

Those who lived by the "belief" that the earth was flat had the ground cut out from under them by Columbus.

Those who lived by the "belief" that the earth was the center of the universe, as was believed in Biblical times, had the ground cut out from under them by Galileo and Copernicus.

Those who lived by the "belief" that Homo sapiens was actually, literally, created in a literal Garden of Eden had the ground cut out from under them by Darwin.

A barrier to religious growth is the inability to differentiate between "belief" and "faith." A genuine and authentic faith is beyond belief. Faith begins where belief ends. Faith is the antithesis of belief.

The person who lives by "beliefs" is in the continually precarious position of having the ground cut out from under him by some new discovery of science or by some new result of scholastic research.

The point is: Beliefs have to be in a state of continual change to be kept in harmony with new discoveries and insights. *But not so with faith.* Nothing learned, discovered, taught, written or thought by man can bother or threaten the person who understands the nature of faith.

We are not "saved" through proper "believing" of certain theological propositions or speculations. But from the beginning of Biblical literature to the end, there is a theme, there is a chord, there is a proclamation.

It runs from the anguished cry of Job: "Though God slay me, yet will I retain my faith in Him." It swells in crescendo through the teachings of Jesus. "Thy faith has made thee well — never have I seen such faith," Jesus said time and time again. Paul picks up the theme in these words: "By grace you have been saved through faith."

Faith comes with the discovery of the holy dimension of our existence. It is the realization that our life is related to the ultimate. When we experience that dimension of existence, we will have moved beyond belief, in freedom, to faith.

To have a living faith in a living God means that we can, comfortably, in freedom, move into tomorrow with all of the risks and the uncertainties. "Time makes ancient good uncouth; they must upward and onward who would keep abreast of truth," wrote James Russell Lowell in the great hymn, *Once to Every Man and Nation.*

Truth is never static or crystallized. Revelation will tolerate no perfect tense.

One who understands the nature of faith can move onward and upward into the unknown and uncharted wilderness ahead with a living faith in a living reality that IS, not WAS.

To live and to die in such a faith is to experience the reality of living in grace, this grace that is the most enriching, fulfilling and beautiful experience on this planet Earth.

This grace is greater than religion, greater than theology, greater than the Church.

Greater than the Bible even, is this grace that is experienced by one who lives in such faith. To have experienced such a grace, through this faith that is beyond belief, is to have already experienced your own resurrection.

God Doesn't Need Protection

Federal Judge Learned Hand (1872-1961) has been regarded by many as the greatest American jurist of our time. He had no superior in the jurisprudence of the English speaking world.

The Spirit of Liberty is a collection of his papers and addresses. It is a classic of clear thought. His words have fed my mind and spirit for over 20 years. In an address on "The Principles of Civil Liberties and Human Rights" are these words: "It is only by trial and error, by insistent scrutiny, doubting and questioning, by the readiness to re-examine presently accredited conclusions that we have risen, so far as in fact we have risen, from our brutish ancestors. All discussion, all debate, all dissidence, tends to question, and in consequence to upset existing convictions: that is precisely its purpose and its justification. The only chance for truth to emerge is a fair field for ALL ideas.

"But how many of us try to suppress arguments that disturb our complacency, and yet to continue to congratulate ourselves on keeping the faith.

"Heretics have been ostracized and exiled, but it is impossible to smother them. And so, if I am to say what are the principles of civil liberties and human rights, I answer that they lie in the habits and customs that tolerate and encourage dissent and are ready to overhaul existing assumptions, and even to undertake the intolerable labor of thought, that most distasteful of all of our activities."After 50 years in the Christian church and 25 years as an ordained Christian minister serving both Presbyterian and Congregational churches, I am still continually startled and amazed at the numbers that are sent into trauma and incoherency, by any questioning of their "beliefs." How threatened they must be. How precariously thin their "faith." How 'shaky" the "truth" they live by. The nerves touched by observations made in this column only once again confirm how insecure so many are who "congratulate themselves on keeping the faith," in Judge Hand's words.

Perhaps this accounts for such sloppy and careless reading. An example: my "reincarnation" column. Not once did I say that reincarnation was "Christian" nor that I personally believed in it. I merely said at the very beginning that the subject was one of the most interesting in the study of religions. My statement that some dogmatic and narrow Christians may have to come back again and learn a little humility was stated "tongue in cheek" that anyone reading it carefully recognized and appreciated. The important question that strikes at the heart of the matter is this: Why should surveying a short history of reincarnation have been so threatening to those "congratulating themselves on keeping the faith?" By contrast, those not threatened found it "one of the most interesting columns they had read."

The nationally syndicated columnist Sydney Harris once made a profound observation: "If someone derives an emotional advantage from misunderstanding you, there is no way you are ever going to make yourself understood."

The Rev. Dr. Leslie Weatherhead, who for years was the beloved pastor of the famed City Temple of London, and whose books have been read by millions, wrote one of his best, *The Christian Agnostic.* The idea being that anyone within Christianity (especially a minister or teacher) who is not an agnostic, a doubter and a questioner is dangerous. An agnostic is one who can say in all humility, as he stands before unanswerable questions, "I don't know."

In the absence of agnosticism, questioning, searching and seeking, you have the narrow dogmatism of the closed mind. Agnosticism indicates that a teacher has reckoned with realities and that he knows and recognizes the limitations of his intellect. It is not a denial of anything. It is just a humble recognition of our total inability to answer questions having to do with the creation, its origins, its purpose, and its destiny. Therefore, anyone who suggests to me that God will not stand up unless sheltered from inquiry, I can only stare at in wonderment. Anyone who suggests to me that God is not safe unless defended from nonbelievers and questioners, I look upon with pity.

I think God (he, she or it) needs no protectors. I have often wondered why so many are so nervous about God . . . and seem to feel that their "faith" must in every way be protected. They must be continually reminded that "In God We Trust" or presumably they might relax and stop trusting. The *true believer* "congratulating himself on keeping the faith" must feel he is saving God from extinction.

I would think, in my quieter and more rational moments, that such "believers" might come to the realization that if his God or his "faith" needed this much protection, something is wrong. What kind of a God or a "faith" could it be that would be so dependent on the Rev. Mr. John Doe's protection?

Why cannot we simply say: "We honestly do not know the answers, but the only chance for truth to emerge is a fair field for all ideas." In our quest together, perhaps we can grow and unfold toward that mystery and that kingdom "where not even a sparrow falls to the ground unknown, and where the least shall be considered side by side with the greatest."

What do we know? Only this: that we have the same needs and are all brothers and sisters. Come then, let us bow our heads before the eternal thou, the divine rhythm, before the mystery, the divine flow of the universe that we call God, and then let us rise up and help each other as we pass upon our way.

Conceptions Of God Fall Woefully Short

The brilliant philosopher-mathematician Alfred North Whitehead said: "The most important question facing modern man and woman is, 'What do you mean by God?'"

Few words are tossed around so loosely by clergy and laity alike. Words are symbols. The symbolic nature of language is often ignored or unknown. The three letters, G-O-D, are only a symbol of what: a *he*, a *she*, an *it*, a *metaphysical abstraction*, a *principle*, a *divine blur*, a *what*?

Not too many years ago, a survey was done on this question by several national Protestant denominations. Grade school children in Sunday school were asked: "How do you think of God?" Then, church-attending adults were asked exactly the same question.

The answers given by the adults, with very few exceptions, were almost exactly the same as the answers of the grade school children. Only the choice of words was different. "God" was thought of as a divine window-peeker — always *watching* what we do. Until only recently a religious order of women was required to wear robes in their shower bath so that, according to the order's rule, "The good God could not see them nude."

"God" was thought of as a cosmic bellhop, just waiting for our call and requests so that he could deliver the order. "God" was also thought of as a celestial hit man, who decided to *take* little Johnny one day, Ruth the next, and so forth; or a heavenly magician who can *do tricks* with nature and natural law. And the grotesque images of the *mystery* behind this cosmos continued on in that vein.

In a poetic satire, W. H. Auden writes about whose who bombard the heavens with words based on such images:

"O God, put away justice and truth, for we do not want them. Leave thy heavens and come down to our earth of water clocks and hedges. Become our nice uncle . . . Look after baby . . . amuse Grandfather . . . Escort Madam to the opera and be sure and help Willy with his homework. Introduce Muriel to some nice, handsome naval officer . . . and we will love you . . . as we love ourselves."

A few years ago. Dr. Nathan Pusey, president of Harvard University, said this in a baccalaureate sermon:

"When one considers how inadequately churches have spoken to people in this new age, it is not surprising that so many have withdrawn from, or remain outside churches. Among the major failures of the traditional Christian church is the continual presentation of juvenile conceptions of God, primitive superstitious notions of a large-sized man who exists to be pleased like an old style father, a fickle judge, or at best some kind of anthropomorphic figure whose conduct could be compared to that of our own more virtuous human beings."

In a universe composed of thousands of galaxies, with vastness of space and time beyond all human comprehension, thousands upon thousands of clergy and laity on a little speck called "Earth" will Sunday after Sunday tell you what the "God" behind and within all of this wants you to do, wants you to think, and "expects" of you.

These same clergy and laity cannot even explain a lightbulb or a radio, and yet they will tell you, in what must be the ultimate arrogance, what the "mystery" behind this cosmos is and wants. They will define "God" for you while standing speechless before the complications of a radio. All talk as to the *nature* of "God" seems to me to be incredibly naive in a universe of such magnitude, such time and space dimensions beyond all comprehension. Our little Earth is only a speck of sand on the cosmic beach.

A few of the Hebrew prophets had an intuitive insight to this when they wrote of a God "whom no man hath seen or can ever see. We know him not." They wrote, "His greatness is unsearchable."

"To DEFINE God is to *deny* him," wrote Spinoza. Even in John Calvin's day the Rev. Richard Hooker wrote, "Our soundest knowledge of God is to know that we know him not . . . as he is . . . and our safest eloquence concerning him is our silence, when we confess without confession that his greatness is above our capacity and reach."

Is it not true that a God understood would be no God at all? To think that *God is as we think of him* would be nothing short of blasphemy? To leave God *unknown* and *unnamed* is *not* to lose God. Silence names as well as sound; whatever is behind this cosmos and through all, and in all, is *in* us.

Thoreau once commented that he was sure "God would prefer us to be atheistic than to believe all of the grotesque images that have been presented to us."

Definitions of God have been vanishing, idols have been tumbling, symbols have been falling away, trinities have been dissolving, religious personalities have been waning, but the *eternal reality* still moves throughout the cosmos.

We can still say that this *ultimate reality* is a cosmic love of which our little human loves are only a small part. We can experience it partly throughout human love, still trusting the love of the ultimate reality is deeper and more divine than human reason can fathom.

This *ultimate reality* . . .
"In the blush of every dawn,
in the evening breeze,
in the leaf's low murmur,
the swell of the oceans and the seas,
the rising and ebbing of the tide,
the mote in the sunbeam."

"Creation's ascent and fall . . .

54

the link . . . the chain of existence . . .
beginning and end of all . . .
artist of the solar spaces and of human faces . . .
though all human races claim thee . . .
thought and language fail to name thee . . .
mortal lips be dumb before thee . . .
silence . . .
only . . .
can adore . . .
thee."

THE BIBLE

"The 'Bible' before it was 'bible' was first cult prescriptions . . . cult prescriptions later on acquire a sacred authority from the intimacy of their association with the rites of the cult."

"Before the invention of the printing press . . . no two copies of a book were ever alike . . . ante-printing press translations were slow and inevitably erroneous."

"Greek manuscripts of the Old Testament were edited to make them conform more explicitly to the Christian faith. They were also edited to make them conform with current liturgical practices."

"When a person reads Hemingway, he is reading Hemingway . . . but when he reads the Bible he is NOT READING THE BIBLE (the originals), but he is only reading a translation of a translation of a translation of a translation . . . of a translation . . . ad infinitum."

"The inaccuracy of the King James Bible makes it impossible for any serious student to use that version in any serious study."
  – Ernest Cadman Colwell, Ph.D., former Dean, the Theological Seminary, Chicago University, and former President, University of Chicago

How Can Every Bible Translation Be Infallible?

Dr. James Bennet Pritchard is one of the most distinguished Biblical scholars and archaeologists in the world. He is professor emeritus of Religious Studies at the University of Pennsylvania and curator of the Near Eastern section of the University museum. He is Biblical advisor to *National Geographic* magazine, the *British Broadcasting System,* and *Time-Life Books;* and past president of the Archeological Institute of America.

Several years ago, he was invited to the University of Puget Sound in Tacoma, Washington, as distinguished lecturer and scholar for a year. His series of lectures to overflow audiences was on "The Bible Today."

He ended his first lecture with these words: "If these discoveries and developments had not taken place, many would have been more comfortable, and they could still read the Bible as did their fathers and grandfathers a century ago. But *that is no longer possible.* The discoveries *have* been made and reported by honest and scholarly men and women. We have been cast out of the mythical Garden of Eden. An angel with the flaming sword of knowledge blocks the way of ever again returning to that Bible our grandparents read."

The next day the switchboard at the university was flooded with indignant callers asking: "Why did the university let that man come and say all of those things about 'our' Bible?"

The people calling, I am sure, had "studied" the Bible to just about the same depth and degree as my cat. They think "reading" an English translation is "studying" the Bible, without any regard for all of the complexities of the Hebrew and Greek languages, the translation and transmission problems, combined with the historical, religious, archaeological and sociological implications of the times that produced the material.

Dr. Gerald Kennedy, the youngest senior bishop in the history of the Methodist Church preached one of his greatest sermons on this subject, titled, "Playing a Game Called 'Church.'"

In his Tacoma lecture, Pritchard discussed archaeological discoveries, plus a greater understanding of Hebrew words and terms, unknown in the past which are now understood. The recovery of artifacts, tablets, scrolls and so forth have all contributed to great knowledge of Biblical material. The highly sophisticated dating methods they work with today make the old Carbon-14 dating tests look almost archaic.

And yet today, in 1983, we still have those who claim the Bible is "infallible," that is "without error" of any kind. It is beyond belief. I used to make this point by going into Bible book stores, asking the salesperson if he or she believed the Bible to be "infallible, without errors?" If they replied in the affirmative, I would then say, "Well I was just looking over your Bible shelf and there are 10 different translations, all using different words and expressions. Would you please come over and show me which of the 10 is the 'infallible, without error' translation?

"Quite obviously all 10 cannot be without error, since entirely different words and concepts are used, and I want to read only the one that is 'without error.'" That usually ended the discussion.

There has never been found an original manuscript of any book in the Bible. All anyone has ever had are copies, literally copies of copies of copies — translations of translations of translations. Before the printing press was invented in the 15th Century, no two translations were ever alike.

The production of books or translations was exceedingly slow and inevitably erroneous. Translators made many, many mistakes. And, in addition to the mistakes, translators would often change the text to conform with their own view, or their own theology.

To have an infallible Bible, the 1,300 years of oral tradition would have had to be passed down infallibly after being infallibly started. And then, after 1,300 years of infallible oral tradition, you would have needed thousands of infallible translators. Then, after the thousands of infallible translators, you would still need an infallible interpreter, or an infallible reader to infallibly interpret the infallible translations. Then, of course, considering the dozens and dozens of various translations on the newsstand today, you have to ask which one is the infallible translation today, assuming you feel you can read infallibly.

In the *Laymen's Theological Library* series, an excellent non-denominational study, Dr. Fred Denbeaux of Union Theological Seminary said it all in these words: "The person who is unwilling to study linguistics, history and literature cannot ever *understand the Bible.* The Bible is a most difficult book; it is a book that has been used to sustain every conceivable form of bigotry, ignorance, superstition and darkness. No true scholar is ever afraid to be a critic of the Bible. He realizes that far from being destructive, it is *the only honestly constructive approach there is, as it is a seeking for truth.*"

What you and I do with the Bible, after honestly studying the research of the most eminent scholars available, is up to us. It is up to the individual to decide how to read it, and how best to use it. But first, if we are going to use it in any enlightened sense, it is just mandatory to know what it is we are reading. Otherwise, in Methodist Bishop Gerald Kennedy's words, "We are simply playing the game called 'church'."

Ten Commandments:
A Cultic Code Of Taboos

No one has so put the Ten Commandments in perspective better than the famous actress Ruth Gordon, probably without even realizing it. She said to an audience: "There is one commandment I have never broken . . . I can assure you. I have never coveted my neighbor's wife."

Perhaps few other parts of the Bible have been so misused, misinterpreted, misunderstood as have the Ten "Commandments." They were a cultic taboo code written BY Hebrew men FOR Hebrew men. Nothing more and nothing less.

Sir James Frazer in his classic *The Golden Bough* writes: "These commandments of Israel are taboos of a familiar type in primitive religions disguised as commands of the tribal god." Dr. Ernest Colwell, former Dean of the Theological Seminary, Chicago University, writes: "These were prescriptions written only for the Hebrew cult. They acquired authority due to their association with the rites of the cult."

All "thou shalt not kill" meant is that thou shall not kill another Hebrew. The giver of the commandment, Moses, quite obviously totally ignored it with everyone except the Hebrews. And all with the jealous tribal God's blessing. In the book of *Numbers*, Chapter 31, verses 17 and 18, Moses himself gives this order, "Now kill every male among the little ones, and kill every woman that hath known a man by lying with him. But all the women children, that have not known a man by lying with him, keep alive for yourselves." Probably in all of history there has never been a command any more revolting to human sensibilities; kill every male and every woman not a virgin, but the virgins keep for yourselves. And in verse 7, it reads: "As God commanded Moses, they killed them all." Quite obviously "Thou shalt not kill" was not understood either by Moses or the Israelites or "God" to be any kind of a moral or ethical prohibition of killing. And so today we still hand out free Bibles to our servicemen going into battle to kill every one of the "enemy" in sight. At least for all the years I was a Marine Corps pilot we were given free Bibles. I assume they still are being given.

According to the Christian fundamentalists, at the same time they are extolling the virtue of the commandment "Thou shalt not kill," they claim that they would have been deprived of salvation if Jesus had not been killed. In other words, through the violation of the commandment they claim that the human race was saved. What double talk they live with.

The commandments that present day sexual moralists like to quote had nothing at all to do either with sex or sexual morality. Nothing could have been further from their minds. These were taboos based on rights of property. Women in this day were owned possessions. The men could sell them or divorce them at will. The men could have both wives and concubines. The greatest of them all, we are told, King Solomon, had more than 700 wives and 300 concubines. Adultery would hardly have been a temptation. With 1,000 women at his disposal there would not be enough hours in the day, or his lifetime. A Hebrew man's real estate, his cattle, his land and his wives were owned property and please note that the wives came after the real estate.

Space precludes documenting each commandment. The majority of the commandments are saturated with what is known in primitive religions as "sympathetic magic." The law of sympathy is "what happens to one will happen to all." For instance, primitive people believed that if a jealous god were angry with one member of a family, then the entire family would be contaminated, and punishment would be inflicted upon all. The taboos against mentioning names and making images was due to the fact that a person could be "sympathetically" injured through naming names or making images of gods.

The word covet, in "Thou shalt not covet (what a man owns)," is all sympathetic magic. The word covet has nothing to do with envy, but more literally means to "cast a spell" (sympathetic magic). Covetous thoughts would call into existence evil spirits, which would cause the loss of a man's possessions. No one was truly safe from such witchcraft; it was therefore feared. The anthropologist Levy-Bruhl writes on this: "Covetousness is of itself not a feeling of desire, but it was thought to have a positive and effectual action of the soul of him who 'covets' upon the thing coveted." A Hebrew word for covet means most literally a "poisoner," "to cast a 'spell'." Quite simply, witchcraft.

Kishif, another Hebrew word meaning coveter, is defined as witchcraft in the Talmud. In many languages, the words coveting, sickness, death and the evil eye are synonymous. The way people read the commandments today is far, far removed from what they meant at the time and why they were even written. There is no connection between them and any moral or ethical code for our time.

To take a superstitious cultic code of taboos from a primitive people of 3,000 years ago, and attempt to make it a divine code of morals for today is nothing short of ludicrous. If we really lived by and as the commandments were written, we would be buried in witchcraft, sympathetic magic, superstition, sorcery and taboos. I hardly think that is what those quoting the commandments today have in mind.

It may be right not to kill anyone instead of just another member of your own race and ethnic group. It may be right to respect all things owned by your neighbor, but it is not the cultic taboo code of a 3,000 year old primitive tribe that makes it right and good. Rather, it is your own innate, humane, moral and ethical sensibilities and sensitivities today that makes it right and good, and that is quite enough.

Love is above manmade cultic codes. Few have said it in more beautiful and meaningful words than the theologian Paul Tillich. "Only the principle of love can recreate continually new guidelines in a changing world. Love alone can transform itself according to the demands of individuals in individual situations without losing its unconditional validity. Only love is eternally flexible and eternally relevant."

The Influence Of Earlier Religions

I do not want to set a precedent by spending an entire column documenting the research and homework that goes into the preparation of these thoughts. I am making an exception today because of the serious nature of the material, as set forth in my column of October 24, the influence of Zoroastrianism on Judaism, Christianity, and Islam.

In addition, there was the interest indicated by the two letters on the subject in The October 31 *Idaho Statesman.*

From *The Encyclopedia of Religion,* The Philosophical Library, New York, "Zoroaster's date of birth, approximately 1000 B.C."

From *Ancient Religions,* edited by Vergilius Ferm, The Philosophical Library: "Although legend places the birth of Zoroaster as far back as 3000 B.C. it would be more accurate to place the event from 1000 to 800 B.C."

From the *Interpreters Bible* in 12 volumes, Abingdon Press, by more than 40 contributing scholars from the major theological schools of our time: "The struggle (between good and evil) is similar to other creation myths such as the Babylonian story of Marduk and Tiamat. There is a closer relationship to the Persian (Zoroastrian) belief of conflicts between the forces of 'good' and 'evil'" (Volume 12).

Again, from Volume 6: "Of special importance is the fact that in *Zechariah (3:1-2)* there appears for the first time in the Old Testament a reference to 'satan.' The date: 522-486 B.C." That is considerably later than Zoroastrianism.

From *Harpers Bible Dictionary,* Harper and Bros. "There is a marked development of the idea of Satan due to Persian influence. The Persians had an elaborate angelology and demonology, and much of it passed into later Jewish thought."

From *Dictionary of the Bible,* Volume 4, Charles Scribners and Sons: "The name and concept of Satan belongs to the *post* exilian age of Hebrew development, fostered by the Persian influence. In Zoroastrianism, the dualism of good opposed to evil is more accentuated than in any other ancient system, Zoroastrian influence largely affected Jewish concepts of Satan, and later Christian."

From *The Columbia Encyclopedia,* Columbia University Press: "The idea of Satan in the Old and New Testaments is closely related to ancient religions of the East, Egyptian and Zoroastrian. Satan can be traced back to pre-Christian deities. Zoroastrianism affected Judaism during the time of the captivity, and later Christianity. The Dead Sea Scrolls strongly reflect Zoroastrian influence."

From *Religions in Four Dimensions,* Walter Kaufman, Princeton University, (section on the subject matter): "The influence of Zoroastrianism on Christianity and Judaism has been *immense.* Many of the central notions of both were adopted from Zoroastrianism. We ask, where do the Christian concepts of angels, satan, hell, paradise come from. The answer is, in one word, Zoroaster. Christianity followed Zoroaster in dividing humanity into two camps, the followers of 'truth' and the followers of the 'lie.' The manner in which the New Testament authors put the word 'truth' into the sayings of Jesus is entirely Zoroastrian. An example from the *Gospel of John:* 'I have come into the world to bear witness to the truth. Everyone who is of the truth hears my voice.' The use of the word 'truth' here is entirely Zoroastrian."

From *Occidental Mythology,* Viking Press, Joseph Campbell (whom the *New York Times* last year called "the most eminent religious historian and mythologist alive today"): "The progress that oriental scholarship has made toward an understanding of the relationship between Zoroastrianism and Christianity is secure and convincing. The great themes of Zoroaster can be heard echoed and re-echoed in Greek, Hebrew, Arabic and every tongue of the West."

From *Religions of the World,* G. L. Berry, Barnes and Noble publisher: "In Zoroastrianism, the spirit of 'good' was Mazda, Lord of Wisdom, with his helper Mithras, light. Mithraism (outgrowth of Zoroastrianism) was adopted in large part by Christian teachings and ritual. On the judgment day, all non-believers would perish, the good would inherit the world of peace and 'paradise' forever. Since Mithras was a sun-god, sun-day was automatically sacred to him and called 'the Lord's day,' hundreds of years before Jesus.

"On Dec. 25, there were elaborate celebrations with hymns being sung and sacraments of bread and wine administered. Between Dec. 25 and the spring equinox (Easter) came the mystical 40 days of search, which was the origin of Christian lent. Mithras, and later Jesus, was described as 'the Way,' 'the Truth,' 'the Son of God,' 'the Light,' 'the Life,' 'the Word,' as well as 'the Good Shepherd.' Mithras was often represented as carrying a lamb on his shoulders, just as Jesus at a later period."

From *Our Oriental Heritage,* Volume I (of 12 volumes) by Will Durant, Simon and Schuster publisher: "One hears, in Christian theology, as many echoes of Persian Zoroastrianism as of Hebrew thought and Greek philosophy. All 'good' men will join the god Mazda in 'paradise.'"

I could continue with a hundred more references from scholars in every major university or theological seminary in the world. In every good library can be found dozens of excellent references documenting the influence of earlier religions on the later religions of Judaism, Christianity and Islam.

This really is nothing new.

It is as old as scholarship.

And as old as . . . academic and intellectual integrity.

Seek Holy Myths That Live,
Not Just Survive

One of the highlights of my life was studying four summers ago under Joseph Campbell. Last year, in a *New York Times Magazine* interview, Campbell was described as "the pre-eminent scholar in the world today in religious history and mythology." Bill Moyer's recent interview with him confirmed that judgment.

I always made it mandatory that my university students submit a paper on "The Role of Mythology in Religious Ritual and Literature." The phrase "Comparative Religions" is really not used too much any more at the university level. We use the phrase "Comparative Mythologies."

There is no way to study or understand religion intelligently without a thorough understanding of mythology and mythological symbolism. Basic mythological themes have been present everywhere; and either by diffusion or as a part of our collective experiences, they appear and reappear with only slight variations to meet local needs.

The comparative study of mythologies compels us to view the cultural history of mankind as a unit because there are universal mythological themes. Examples are the deluge or flood, land of the dead, virgin birth, resurrected hero, the sacred meal, or ritualistic cannibalism (the belief that men acquired the powers of whatever organism they consumed, so by eating the body of a god, they shared in the god's attributes and powers). Such themes are universal and have appeared everywhere in various combinations, yet remain basically the same.

No human society has yet been found in which such mythological motifs have not been rehearsed in liturgies, presented in art, and magnified in song. Every people has received its own seal and sign of the supernatural communicated to its heroes.

The tragic and misleading situation lies in trying to read mythological symbols as *historical fact*. When mythology is misread as history, metaphor becomes dogma. And symbols become petrified into creeds. Example: The phrase, "Jesus ascended into heaven and sitteth at the right hand of God . . ." read historically, literally and factually becomes absurd.

Are we to imagine a human body rising from this earth, passing beyond the bounds of this solar system, beyond the bounds then of the Milky Way, beyond the bounds next of our super galaxy, and beyond the bounds even of what may be beyond that?

So we ask, "At what velocity is the body moving?" It must still be in flight and still ascending if we are to read the account historically and literally. Let us assume the body is ascending at the speed of light (which for a physical body would be impossible). Having been launched less than 2,000 years ago, even if the body were traveling and ascending at this phenomenal speed, the body would still not even be out of our own galaxy. Such images are meaningless and absurd outside of the symbolism of mythology. With the body of Jesus still ascending, where is it headed?

Or let me put it another way. To attempt to read resurrection stories as physical and literal presents a problem that even the official philosopher of the Roman Catholic Church, St. Thomas Aquinas, could not think his way through. He thought and thought about a very grave problem that modern theologians have not given enough attention to. Here is a cannibal, he imagines, who has never eaten anything but human flesh and whose father and mother before him had never eaten anything but human flesh. Every particle of his body rightfully belongs to someone else.

Now, we cannot suppose that those eaten by cannibals are to be rejected in heaven for eternity. But if not, what then is left of the cannibal? How can he be roasted in hell after all of his body is restored to its original owners? You can see the absurdity of attempting to interpret mythological, spiritual symbols as literal, historical facts.

An important distinction must be made too between *living* myths and mythological symbols that are artificially retained and are archaic. The first function of a living mythology (and I repeat *living* mythology) and mythic rituals is to waken in the individual a sense of awe, wonder, and a participation in the mystery of being. Living myth does that, but not myth that is being artificially retained.

A *living* myth leads to the source, to the spirit, to the holy, to the mystery. Whereas those myths that are artificially retained and have long since lost their significance, lead only to support an institution.

What is a *living* myth? Where everything and every daily activity and every moment of every waking hour is oriented around the symbols that point to the holy and the mystery.

Dr. Howard Moody is the senior minister of the well known Judson Memorial Church of New York City. For years he had wanted to take a sabbatical leave and live and study with a Navajo holy man. His church granted him a six-month leave for such a venture. He writes that there was nothing in his 50 years in the Christian church nor his 25 years of Christian ministry that prepared him for such a spiritual pilgrimage . . . to live with people where myth was reality, where every aspect of existence is touched by the unseen spirit, and is sacred.

Consequently he wrote these words: "My Christian theology seemed shriveled and incomplete and I knew I would never again be the same after the profoundly beautiful spiritual experience of living with these holy people and their holy men."

Living myth points you to the spirit, to the mystery, the holy, the source. Living myth does not lead to an institution.

Today we must allow our spirit to soar and fly in the timeless, spaceless quest for the source of the holy. The quest has been described many times in different ways in the myths of mankind. We must describe our own.

"Archaeological discoveries and research render OBSOLETE much that has been written about the Biblical patriarchs."

"The Biblical picture of Solomon's 'greatness' was only an 'idealization' of the past by a depressed LATER generation . . ."

The poetic form of Canaanite mythology in the Canaanite Bible from PRE-Israelite days is strikingly similar to that employed by the writers of the Psalms."

"Before the Israelites there were the far more sophisticated and culturally advanced Canaanites. And a very high culture had even preceded the Canaanite, the Chalcolithic period."

"Basic ideas found in the New Testament, like Messianic expectation, are now documented as having been current in Jewish thought of the First Century . . . at the time of writing the New Testament."

> *– James Bennet Pritchard, Ph.D.,*
> *Professor Emeritus of Religious*
> *Studies, University of*
> *Pennsylvania; Curator of the Near*
> *Eastern section of the museum;*
> *Archaeological Advisor to the*
> *National Geographic, Time-Life*
> *Books, the British Broadcasting*
> *Corporation and Reader's Digest*

Myths And Religion

Bill Moyers had two interviews with Joseph Campbell for his national television program, *Bill Moyers' Journal.* In his introduction Moyers said "Joseph Campbell is one of the world's foremost scholars of mythology." Anyone having an interest in becoming religiously educated and enlightened will be helped by insights from these interviews.

Campbell brings out, of course, that mythological themes or motifs such as flood, virgin birth, resurrected hero, "heaven" concepts, a sacred meal (or ritualistic cannibalism) have a world-wide distribution and are everywhere. They are organized and ritualized according to local needs. In the Moyers' interview, Campbell said, "When people try to interpret a spiritual symbol (in mythology) as though it referred to a concrete fact, you have lost the message."

Moyers: "Give me an example."

Campbell: "Well, the image of the virgin birth is perfect for an example. This is a motif that occurs in all the mythologies of the world. There are virgin births all over the place in all religions. 'Virgin birth' is symbolic of the birth of the spiritual life, and so with resurrection themes or motifs. Misunderstanding consists in reading spiritual mythological symbols as though they were references to historical, factual events."

Other observations by Campbell in the interviews include the following: "The 'hero' in mythology is always the founder of something, a new religion, a new age, a new way of life. The 'hero' founders of all religions usually go on their vision quest. The Buddha went into solitude and sat beneath the tree of Immortal Knowledge; Jesus goes off into the desert for 40 days; Zoroaster goes off into the desert, and so it goes. And you might say the founder of one's own life instead of living everybody else's life, must come from a quest too.

"Throughout the inhabited world, in all times and under every circumstance, the myths of man have flourished, and they have been the living inspiration of whatever else may have appeared on the activities of the human body and mind. It would not be too much to say that myth is the secret opening through which the inexhaustible energies of the cosmos pour into human cultural manifestation: Religions, philosophies, arts, and the social forms of primitive and historic man.

"The motivating force that has elevated man from the ground dwelling apes is the sense of awe and mystery, which is the first function of mythology, and it is that that carries him on. This is the mystical function that makes a connection between our waking consciousness and the mystery of the universe. The second function of myth gives us a picture of the universe. It allows us to see ourselves in relationship to nature, as when we speak of Father Sky and Mother Earth. The third function of myth is sociological, in that it supports a social order; and lastly myth has a psychological function in that it offers a way of passing through, and dealing with, the various stages of life from birth to death.

"It is encouraging that more and more people today are learning to let religious symbols speak directly to them. They are finally realizing that no longer are they going to let a committee of Bishops, or other church 'leaders' meet in a conference and then decide for everyone how the symbols are to be read and interpreted, nor how they must be believed."

Having studied with Joseph Campbell and communicating with him on a regular basis, I can make some personal observations. He is perhaps the most deeply spiritual person, in its most profound sense, that I have ever known. In his lecturing and his presence, there is a radiance, and a quality of peace, harmony and wholeness — a centeredness that I have known in few other people.

He is, without question, the most intellectually brilliant person I have ever heard lecture. The material he has at his command can only be called awesome. For all of his adult life he has indexed and outlined every book he has studied and then committed the outline to memory. He is now 80; looks like he is 50, and lectures and converses with an energy and vitality that people in their 20's would envy.

Two of his favorite words are "awe" and "mystery." And the first function of mythology, all mythologies, whether North American Indian or Christian, is to point us toward the mystery, in awe.

For those wanting to enlarge their understanding of religious mythology, I suggest Campbell's *The Flight of the Wild Gander,* Viking Press; *The Hero With a Thousand Faces,* Princeton University Press (a text used in many university classes in religion); *The Masks of God* in four volumes: *Oriental Mythology, Primitive Mythology, Occidental Mythology,* and *Creative Mythology,* Viking Press; and *The Mythic Image,* Princeton University Press and a magnificent book. It sells for $75, so you may want to go to the public library.

"A living mythology points you toward the source, the holy and the mystery. An artificially retained mythology points you only toward a religious institution."

68

About Reincarnation

One of the most interesting subjects in the study of religions is the widespread belief in reincarnation — that souls have many lives and that you and I "have lived a thousand times and will be born a thousand times again," in the words of Goethe, author of *Faust*.

A great many have the mistaken idea that reincarnation is believed by only a few Hindus. But the list of intellectual giants of the world in all religions (and outside of organized religions) who have believed in reincarnation is long. It includes Leonardo Da Vinci, Paracelsus, Shakespeare, John Donne, Benjamin Franklin, David Hume, Immanuel Kant, Napoleon Bonaparte, Schopenhauer, Victor Hugo, Ralph Waldo Emerson, Thoreau, Walt Whitman, Soren Kierkegaard, Dostoevsky, Henry Ford, Robert Frost, T. S. Eliot, Charles Lindbergh, Thomas Huxley, Julian Huxley, Thomas Edison, Luther Burbank, Plato, Albert Schweitzer, The Rev. Dr. Leslie Weatherhead of London's City Temple . . . I could continue for 20 pages. All have written of their belief or interest in reincarnation.

Even more surprising to many is that the Old and New Testaments are filled with reincarnation statements.

In the first century, the Jewish Historian, Flavius Josephus, matter of factly wrote of reincarnation in his famed work, *The Jewish War:* "Do you not know that those who depart of this life are again sent back into pure bodies?" And there is much more. The Essenes taught the soul's pre-existence and continued rebirth.

In the Jewish Kabala, reincarnation is an essential part of the system. According to the *Universal Jewish Encyclopedia*, reincarnation is a universal belief in Hasidism. Martin Buber devoted a great deal of his life to spreading its teachings.

How general was the belief in reincarnation is evidenced by the statement in New Testament literature that the prophets had returned again.

In *Matthew 16:13-14*, for example, Jesus asks his disciples, "Who do men say that I the Son of man am?" And they replied, "Some say that you are John the Baptist (who had already been beheaded), some say you are Elijah and others say you are Jeremiah, or one of the prophets *returned.*"

In Chapter 17:9-13, the disciples remind Jesus that Elijah would come again and restore things. Jesus tells them that Elijah had already come back. The disciples understood this to mean reincarnated in John the Baptist.

St. Paul in *Ephesians 1:4* speaks of mankind as having had pre-existent souls: "God hath chosen us before the foundations of the world."

Space precludes the dozens of Biblical references to reincarnation and pre-existent souls, but two more are noteworthy.

In *John 9:1-3*, concerning the man who had been born blind, they asked Jesus, "Who did sin, this man, or his parents, that he was born blind?" Obviously, if a man had been born blind his sin could not have been committed in this life. Belief in reincarnation is taken for granted in the question.

And Paul writes that "God loved one and hated the other before they were born" (meaning Jacob and Esau)." How could a non-existent being be either loved or hated? Pre-existent souls, reincarnation and Karmic law are taken for granted in these statements.

The law of Karma, defined as the moral law of cause and effect, is better understood if we think of it organically in terms of cosmic harmony, which, when disturbed, must be restored. "The heart of it is Love," said Buddha.

Karma implies a completely moral universe and commits those who believe in it to total, complete person responsibility. No more passing the buck as to your condition. You made your bed. You are lying in it. Many of us refer to Karmic law daily with such statements as: "As a man sows, so shall he reap," or "Sow a thought to reap an act, sow an act to reap a habit, sow a habit and reap a character, sow a character and reap a destiny." In reincarnation, a person has the continual opportunity, either in this life or the next time around, to restore the balance and the harmony through personal decisions in freedom.

Belief in reincarnation was widespread among the early church fathers as well. Justin Martyr wrote of "souls inhabiting many bodies." Clement of Alexandria wrote "before the foundation of the world were we, who pre-existed." Origen taught the pre-existence of souls and reincarnation. And the Christian Gnostics were all reincarnationists. In major universities worldwide and in psychiatric centers such as the world famous Menninger's clinic eminent scientists are working with people who, under hypnosis, are giving names, places, dates and events of previous existences. This information is checked out with the most rigorous methods in order to avoid fakery and error. There are thousands of documentations of such cases. Among the most notable is the work done by Dr. Ian Stevenson, the chairman of the Department of Neurology & Psychiatry at the University of Virginia School of Medicine.

There is a refreshing thought in all of this. Those arrogant "Christians" of our own time who presumptuously declare that all of those who do not conform to their definitions of Christian are *not* Christian ... will have to come back in the next life as one persecuted by such dogmatism in order to learn a little humility.

"If a man dies, shall he live again?" asked the biblical Job. For 150,000 years from Neanderthal to Homo sapiens, we have been answering with a resounding yes.

"I have lived a thousand times and I will return a thousand times more," writes the genius, Johann Wolfgang von Goethe, choosing these words for his *Song of the Spirits over the Waters:*

"The soul of man is like to water;
From Heaven it cometh
To Heaven it riseth
And then returneth to earth,
Forever alternating."

"The Gospels are NOT historical documents. It is absolutely certain that early 'Christian' teaching was not written down at all. Among the 12 disciples . . . probably none of them . . . or one or two at the most . . . could even write."

> – Daniel-Rops, French Catholic
> scholar, from <u>Jesus and His Times</u>

"The truth is . . . it is not a 'historical' Jesus . . . but the 'spirit' of Jesus that is significant for our time."

> – Albert Schweitzer

"A major change came about in my life at one point. Up to then I had been CONDITIONED . . . both lovingly and harshly to live in accord with inspirations . . . values . . . biases . . . concepts . . . resolves . . . laws . . . loyalties . . . and creeds . . . EVOLVED BY OTHERS. From that point on . . . I RESOLVED TO DO MY OWN THINKING."

> – Buckminster Fuller

"Jesus could never have regarded himself as either God or Son of God. Either conception to a Jew is not only impious and blasphemous, but totally incomprehensible."

> – Joseph Klausner, *Jesus of Nazareth,*
> written a generation ago in
> Jerusalem by one of the most
> preeminent Biblical scholars of that
> time

"Imagination would soon begin to weave legends round the figure of Jesus. Disciples would seek to modify them in accordance with their own particular views."

> – T. Henshaw, Ph.D.
> Oxford University

"We know almost nothing about either the life or the personality of Jesus since early Christian sources are fragmentary and legendary."

> – Rudolf Bultmann
> distinguished German theologian

JESUS AND CHRISTIANITY

Distortions Disguise Real Jesus

In my columns, sermons and lectures I often refer to *scholars* for documentation. Surely, if we are at all serious in our religious quest, it is worth our time to give attention to those men and women who have spent a lifetime in related disciplined studies, especially those men and women who are considered *scholars* by the religion departments of major universities and the major theological seminaries.

Unfortunately and far too often, some denominational seminaries are coerced into following a *party line* as opposed to academic integrity. I am thinking of one in particular that was told by the largest financial supporter of that institution that if they did not teach what he considered *proper,* he would withdraw his millions.

Any number of the faculty quit. Many ministers have known the same experience of a biblically and religiously illiterate parishioner who tried to *buy them* saying: "If you do not say what I want to hear, I will withdraw all financial support."

Surely, God must smile upon those ministers and institutions who refuse to prostitute their intellectual and spiritual integrity in the face of economic manipulation.

Now, back to the scholars:

There are many pre-eminent biblical scholars who say that there is no relationship between a Jew, named Jesus, and the *official Christ* of the institutional church.

Soren Kierkegaard, "The Great Dane" as he is known, is studied in every major university and theological seminary in the world. He perhaps put it about as bluntly as it can be said: "Gangs of swindlers have taken forcible possession of the firm of Jesus Christ and have done a flourishing business under the name of Christianity.

This whole thing, is what is known in criminal cases as forgery. And if you doubt me, my friend, all you have to do is read the Gospels about Jesus. The Jesus of the Gospels must be changed and altered drastically to fit the Jesus of official Christianity. The typical sermon about this Jesus is not only pure twaddle, but worse than that, total dishonesty.

"Christianity is played every Sunday. Artists in dramatic robes and costumes make their appearance in artistic buildings and now, dramatically, play Christianity, or in short, play comedy. The preacher lectures about renunciation while he himself is being steadily promoted to bishop." So wrote Soren Kierkegaard, who is recognized as the father of Christian existentialism. And he felt so close to the Jesus of the Gospels that he devoted his life and studies to that Jesus.

Albert Schweitzer's *Quest of the Historical Jesus* is still a classic in biblical studies. Schweitzer wrote: "Jesus claimed none of the things that the church has claimed for him."

Dr. Joseph Klausner, of the University of Heidelberg, wrote in *Jesus of Nazareth:* "Jesus was not a Christian. He was a Jew. Jesus was a product of Palestine and Judaism. Jesus never even dreamed of being a prophet or a messiah to the non-Jews."

The historian Will Durant put it this way: "Paul created a theology about the man Jesus, a man that he did not even know, 50 or more years after the death of Jesus, with complete disregard and neglect for even the sayings that are attributed to Jesus in the synoptic Gospels. The simple teachings attributed to Jesus become lost in the metaphysical fog of Paul's theology."

Dr. Malachi Martin, a former professor at the Pontifical Biblical Institute in Rome with a doctorate in Semitic languages and Oriental history, wrote in his book *Jesus Now:* "This book is a journey through the quagmire of distortions, deformations and illustrations piled around our view of Jesus. If Jesus of Nazareth were to appear in the Vatican of the 20th century or the Riverside Interchurch Center of this day and year, he would have a hard time identifying himself.

"That, though, would not be the greatest difficulty. The greatest difficulty would be that he would find no room. Jesus Caesar is already there, occupying the executive suite, sitting at the green-topped table during the board meetings, entering the sleek, black limo to be whisked to the airport and signing the immaculately typed orders for the government of the Jesus imperium. The Church of Jesus is ruled by Jesus Caesar."

"Fairest Lord Jesus" Isn't The True Image

"The clergy have abused, distorted, twisted and diluted the story of Jesus for centuries," wrote Dr. Harvey Cox several years ago, when he was the Dean of the Theological Seminary, Harvard University.

He continued:

"They have tried to make the story of Jesus over into a legend about a bloodless ascetic; a dreary life denying philosophy of abstaining from practically everything. Now, this has been a little hard to manage in view of the Biblical portrait of Jesus. I wonder, oftentimes, who drew those countless pictures distributed by churches and Sunday schools of a pale, sterile, effeminate Jesus? Those pictures have done more to destroy the real Jesus than 100 of Herod's legends."

That thought brings to my mind the words of one of the most popular hymns in the Christian church, *Fairest Lord Jesus*. Everytime I have tried to sing it I have wondered if the author ever read the life of Jesus in the Gospels. It is pure fantasy. There is no fairest Lord Jesus in the Gospels, "fairer than the meadows, fairer than the moonlight, fairer than the twinkling stars . . ." You almost choke over the perfumed sweetness of it all.

Jesus was no fairest of the fair, no spineless wishy-washy trying to be everyone's friend. You would never hear Jesus singing "smile and the world smiles with you" . . . or hear him say "you can catch more flies with honey than vinegar."

He would never have taken a Dale Carnegie course on "How to Win Friends and Influence People." He would never have been voted "Man of the Year" by the Jerusalem Chamber of Commerce.

To the Pharisees he said, "You vipers . . . you hypocrites . . . you are full of extortion and rapacity. You are like whitewashed tombs . . . you are full of dead men's bones and iniquity."

He said to the religiously pious and self-righteous, "The prostitutes will go into the Kingdom of God before you" (*Matthew 21:31*). (You don't hear many sermons on that text.)

This is the man who responded with anger on many occasions and who walked through the temple and cleaned it out. He had no intention of being everyone's buddy or friend. This is the man who, walking by the sea of Galilee, said to fishermen, "Follow thou me" and they followed him. Can you imagine hard muscled, sunburned, tough fishermen following someone "fairer than the twinkling stars?"

No imperial power wastes time crucifying contemplative, harmless, spiritual mystics. Jesus was killed in the manner of one found guilty of insurrection. "Fairest" people are not killed for insurrection.

Jesus, the man, walks through the pages of the Gospels, hard, sun-tanned, using his powerful hands and feet to do what carpenters had to do in those days. They sat on the floor and held huge beams between their feet, carving massive doors, window frames, roof beams, tables, yokes and plows.

This man, born a Jew, lived a Jew, died a Jew and said repeatedly he was only fulfilling the Jewish religion. Being a Jew means that today Jesus would not be admitted to many of our private clubs. Many of us Christians belong to those clubs and would have to visit with Jesus out on the sidewalk if he dropped by.

Those Jesus chose for friends would have been a terrible offense to many of us sitting in our cozy pews on Sunday mornings: Mary Magdalene, a prostitute; Peter and Andrew, James and John, crude fishermen; Zacchaeus and Matthew, hated tax collectors. He was accused of being a "drunkard and a glutton" *(Matthew 11:19)*, and of "being beside himself." The historian Arnold Toynbee wrote that the people who were involved in the early first century church after the death of Jesus would most closely resemble today those who live in communes and on the streets.

This Jesus never asked anyone what theological creeds they recited, or doctrines they believed, or what communion requirements they approved of, or whether they believed in the trinity or stories about his birth. But time and again, he said only "Thy faith has saved thee. Thy faith has made thee whole."

Faith in whom? Faith in his God.

"Don't call me good," he said; "No one is good but God" *(Mark 10:17)*. He was not praying to himself when he prayed, but to the God of the Hebrews.

This man, Jesus, today would walk the streets and go into the bars, the clubs, the offices and homes to mix with the agnostic, the atheist, the prostitute and tax collector — and those with pious natures would, once again, consider him a great, great offense.

This man, Jesus, would say today, to probably about 90 percent of the Christian church, "Quit this syrupy adulation of me, that is easy. Rather, try something that is hard and very difficult, follow me. Follow me in doing justice, doing righteousness. Follow me in living the Jewish Shema that I gave again as the Great Commandment, 'To love God with all of one's heart and mind, and neighbor as self.' Follow me in doing and living that. That is hard."

Albert Schweitzer, whose doctoral thesis *The Quest for the Historical Jesus* is still a classic, denied the traditional church's doctrine of the divinity of Jesus. Yet Schweitzer wrote from his hospital in the heart of Africa that: "I have spent my entire life following the man who said 'follow thou me.' He comes to us as he came to the fishermen of old, by the lakeside. He says to us the same word 'follow thou me.'"

Many Who Say, "Lord, Lord,"
Ignore Jesus' Message Of Love

What they have done in the past to the beautiful teacher of Galilee is almost beyond comprehension. And, worse, we still continue to this day violating and prostituting both him and his message; or we bury him in theological tombs and roll great stones before the door.

Constantine worshiped the *official Christ* saying, "Lord, Lord," while murdering his own wife, his son and other assorted relatives. Martin Luther worshiped Christ saying, "Lord, Lord," while telling the German aristocracy to cut the throats of the German peasants. He added, "Let there be no half measures. Transfix them. Leave no stone unturned! To kill a rebel is to destroy a mad dog. A prince can enter heaven by the shedding of blood more certainly than by means of prayer."

John Calvin worshiped Christ saying, "Lord, Lord," while burning Servetus at the stake. Ordained ministers worshiped Christ saying, "Lord, Lord," while murdering thousands of so-called witches.

John Wesley worshiped Christ saying, "Lord, Lord," while writing to his wife: "Be content to be insignificant. Of what loss would it be to God or man had you never been born?"

As Albert Schweitzer gave his life, in love, to the sick and the suffering in the heart of Africa, he wrote, "What has been passing for Christianity during these centuries is full of mistakes and horrors. It has not been a Christianity springing from the spirit of love. What Christianity needs is to become a living religion of love. We must lift the spirit of Jesus, which is the spirit of love, from all the trappings of dogma and doctrines created by the theologians of past centuries and let only the spirit of love become central for our lives. To do any little thing in the spirit of love is to live in the spirit of Jesus."

Which is the more difficult choice, to affirm certain theological creeds about Jesus and to repeat a memorized, pat, rote, parrot-like set of beliefs . . . or to live love? The answer seems obvious. Nothing could be easier, or take less effort, than rote-like recitation of memorized cliches and doctrinal creeds that fool us into thinking we are *Christian*. Nothing though could be more difficult than to take the main, primary, recurring theme of love in the teachings of Jesus . . . and *live it*. Nothing in this world is more difficult, demanding or challenging than to *live love*. "Is it a dream . . . ?" Walt Whitman asked. "Nay . . . but the lack of it the dream."

The spirit of Jesus comes to us directly in the impact of life loving life and holding all other life in reverence. It was never praise, adoration or idolizing that Jesus asked for or wanted. Great personalities find that abhorrent. It was simply his cause supported.

He asked that he "be followed," not idolized. Idolization is easy. Following, in the spirit of love, is the most demanding and difficult option we could have been given.

The same words, "Thou shalt love," are said to us today, to be interpreted and made valid in our own time. The same word said to those of old by the lakeside. "Thou shalt love . . . follow me," is said to us. Those who rekindle such a divine and sublime ethic and allow it to burn bright in their own lives, in their own time, will not be far from the Kingdom of God, even as Jesus said. And the "immortal, invisible light inaccessible" no longer will be hidden from our eyes.

"The masculinity of God and of God languages is a cultural and linguistic accident and the masculinity of Christ is on the same order."
> *– Krister Stendahl*
> *Harvard University Divinity*
> *School*

"Nineteenth Century historians REWROTE THE HISTORY of the Revolutionary era to conform with their own Victorian ideals of what women should be . . . and the Nineteenth Century version became the accepted one."
> *– Dr. Linda De Pauw, Professor of*
> *American History, George*
> *Washington University*

"The masses of women who traveled with the Revolutionary armies . . . doing specific work and officially receiving half rations . . . were NOT prostitutes . . . but wives . . . and they were a common sight on the battlefields."
> *– Kathryn Jacob, Archivist*
> *John Hopkins University*

"Whilst you are proclaiming peace . . . good will . . . and freedom and liberty . . . you still insist upon retaining absolute power over Wives."
> *– Abigail Adams (wife of John)*

Jesus Didn't Insult Women;
Why Did Church Fathers?

It seems appropriate to ask the question: "Are women enjoying equal rights with men within Christianity?" Or, could it be said another way. "You've come a long way, baby, except in a large segment of the Christian church where it is men, who speak Sunday after Sunday about 'love,' and how in Christ there is neither male nor female."

William Holladay, professor of Biblical Languages at Andover Newton Theological Seminary, observes that the Bible has been translated by men for men. Their translations are the result of male-centered religious imagery and symbolism. Some examples he makes:

In Hebrew there are words that link a "womb" as the most accurate symbol of God and there are Hebrew words that refer to God as a woman, getting pregnant, having a child and nursing it.

When Moses talked of a God who bore you in the earliest manuscripts, the translators scratched the word "bore" and changed it to "begot." And so, instead of God being a woman who bore you, God became a man who begat you.

He also uses the illustration that countless times in the New Testament Greek words meaning most literally "if anyone" were changed by the translators to read "if a man."

For thousands of years before the Old Testament, female gods reigned supreme in the Near and the Middle East. Her realm extended as far as Spain and India. God became a "man" in Judaism and Christianity.

The Jews came to believe that God had revealed himself as one who had chosen them and they developed a certain ritual which celebrated God's self-revelation. That ritual was circumcision. They came to believe that God dealt primarily with those who were specially marked . . . the circumcised.

Upon arising each day, an Orthodox Jewish male would pray, "I thank thee, O God, that thou has not created me as a woman." As we proceed through the growth and development of Christian dogma and theology, we notice that we have great, so-called, "church fathers," but no one has ever heard of a "church mother."

Let us begin in the third century with one of the first church "fathers," Tertullian, so-called "father" of Western theology. He wrote these words:

"Woman is the Devil's gateway . . . woman is the unsealer of the forbidden tree. Woman was the first deserter of the divine law. It was woman who persuaded the Devil when the Devil was not courageous enough to attack. It was woman who destroyed so easily God's image of man. On account of woman even the Son of God had to die."

81

We move on to Ignatius of Loyola, a church "father," who wrote:

"There is a definite similarity between woman and the Devil. The Devil acts like a woman because he is a weakling."

Or, we move on to church "father" St. Augustine in the fifth century, who wrote that "the image of God was summed up in Adam; and that Eve, taken from Adam's rib, was to serve him forever as a helpmate and was to be used only for the job of reproducing. For any 'spiritual' job only men would be suitable. Woman was not created in the full image of God . . . but ONLY man." She is defined by Augustine as being created ONLY for man. This view still persists.

St. Augustine continues, "A wife is to be totally obedient to her male counterpart," and Augustine saw his own mother as perfectly submissive, who served her husband as Lord and Master, who had no personal rights, either over her mind or her body, and whose husband, father and brother would make all of her decisions for her.

We move on to the 14th century and St. Thomas Aquinas, church "father," who wrote:

"The best a woman can hope for in this or any world is eternal childhood in which she will be subject to man for her own benefit."

Let us move on into the 16th century. In a church report we read the following:

"Woman is far more deceitful than man . . . the reason is that there was a defect in the formation of the first woman, the defect was that she was formed with one of Adam's bent ribs; thus she will always be deceitful, and witchcraft comes from such deceit. Therefore, women are to always be subservient to men."

Still in the 16th century, the Rev. Martin Luther is speaking. This sounds almost like a little third grade boy, mad at some little girl who just beat him in the spelling bee. Luther said, "Men have broad shoulders and large chests, and more understanding (*understanding seems to go with large chests*) so women, therefore, should sit at home . . . be still . . . keep house and bear children."

The 16th century English theologian, Thomas Hooker, put it this way: "Women (*get that . . . women plural, all women, he says*) are inferior, imbeciles by nature, inconstant in mind and infirm in character."

But it was left up to the Rev. John Wesley to add the crowning all-time insult to women — and of all women, to his wife. He wrote the following humiliating, degrading, insulting words:

"Wife, be content to be an insignificant person. Of what importance is your character to mankind? If you were dead and buried right now, or if you had never lived, what loss would it be to the cause of God?"

We could rightly ask, "What kind of a man could write such degrading words to his own wife?" You do not know whether to laugh or cry. When we read such incredible stupidities, it makes one examine other statements made by these "fathers" on other subjects with a far more critical and suspecting eye.

Do you imagine that we are talking only about past times of a bygone day? Is it not true that in our 3,000 years of conditioning as seeing the male as symbolic of religious authority, we think that when a male speaks it has more authority, more truth?

In December 1977, my theological seminary on the campus of Chicago University, held a conference on the role of women in the ministry. It was called "IN CHRIST, NEITHER MALE NOR FEMALE." It was strongly brought to the surface in that symposium that women, no matter how well prepared, no matter how well educated, no matter how academically brilliant, had better be prepared to go jobless, if they are entertaining the illusions that they are going to find a job as a senior preaching minister. You might ask yourself your own feelings privately in your heart, "Would you vote for a woman as your preaching minister?"

Either God speaks to women as to men, or the whole concept of the spirit of God is a mockery and a comedy to puff male ego. Equality of status is not what brings dignity, but equality of opportunity — to be what you are called to be and to do what you are called to do, which applies to all individuals under God, regardless of race, religion or sex.

"Love is not demanding, not jealous. Love is not domineering. Love is not arrogant. In love there is neither male nor female."

It is unique in the sayings attributed to Jesus and the stories of his encounters with women how he places both men and women on the same level of grace, and no lines of superiority or inferiority can be found. Stories of his consideration, his respect, and his tenderness can be found from the Annunciation to the Ascension, from Mary and Martha to Mary Magdalene, to the woman at the well, and to the woman in the house of Simon, which only indicates how far much Christian theology, doctrine and law are removed from the life of Jesus.

One of the most beautiful scenes in the entire Bible is: "There came a woman to the well." As magnificent a picture as I have ever seen was done by a great artist of this one scene. As you look at the picture, all you see is the woman; you can barely see Jesus. His hand is touching hers; the woman is standing by the well. She is so radiant that I cannot describe it. The artist has captured all of the warmth, the beauty of this woman at this point in her life; and in the background, barely visible, is the form of Jesus. Jesus is not the center. The woman is the center. She has become a new, unique person in this living encounter beside this well. And in the Gospel of John at the conclusion of this encounter, it is written that:

"His disciples marveled (*marveled*) that he was talking to a woman," — not just talking to this woman, but any woman! "They marveled that he was talking to a woman."

83

Jesus — As Our Center Point

In *Black Elk Speaks* by John Neihardt, Black Elk says this of the U.S. army's determination to destroy the Sioux: "Our Sioux nation's circle is broken and shattered. There is no center any longer."

Words in T. S. Eliot's *Four Quartets* come to mind:

"At the still point of the turning world . . . at the still point . . . there the dance is . . . Except for the point . . . the still point . . . there would be no dance."

Yeats put it this way: "Things fall apart if the center will not hold . . ."

The still point. The Center. Is it not true that cultures, organizations, individuals must find and hold to some still point?

A world without a center means a people unfulfilled and disoriented. As this is collectively true, so is it individually true. A loss of the still point, the centering point, leads to a fragmented life — lacking wholeness. It is imperative that we as individuals *develop our inner personal center point* to such a degree that it will be a source of stability, an unwobbling source of strength and security.

A potter brings his clay into center on the potter's wheel . . . and then he gives it whatever shape he wishes. Centering is the process of balance. It is that act that precedes all others, the bringing of the clay into a spinning, unwobbling, pivot which will then be free to take many, many shapes.

At the heart of every religion known to me is the thought that there must be the center within us . . . and the center must hold.

Around the stable center there can and will be the dance of life, of celebration. From the holy man of the Oglala Sioux, Black Elk, standing on his holy mountain in South Dakota to the orthodox Christian whose center is the symbol of the Christ dwelling within the heart, to the Taoist whose life is a celebrating dance around the eternal, infinite, inexpressible, centering principle of Tao (the still point is the Tao) . . . for all, the center point is there.

We need to be connected to our center. All activities are connected with our center like rays emanating from a sun. The center is constituted by our most basic convictions, by those ideas which really have the power to move us. The center is where we create an orderly system of ideas . . . our orientation to the world and to our neighbor and to ourselves. Our center regulates the direction of our various strivings.

For many within the Christian community in this Christmas season, the symbol of the Christ is at the still point, in all of its most significant, promising and varied dimensions. Dietrich Bonhoeffer, imprisoned by the Nazis, used these words in talking of his still point, "Christ stands . . . in the center . . . between me and myself . . . the center lying between I and I . . . between I and God . . . between I and my neighbor."

Paul talks about his center point when he makes his prayer, "that Christ may dwell by faith in the heart." The word "heart" here is the Greek word meaning "the core of being," the deepest self, the center, the still point that unites time past and time future.

Jesus provided the center to the life and direction of Albert Schweitzer, who said quite simply, "that anyone who is living in the spirit of love . . . is living in the spirit of Jesus," whether Christian, Jew, Hindu or Buddhist. For Schweitzer the stable, secure, motivating center point of his existence was a Jesus who was the symbol of love. That was it, and all he needed; to live in the spirit of love was to live in the spirit of Jesus. While not believing in any of the traditional orthodox doctrines about Jesus, Schweitzer nonetheless found Jesus the unwobbling center point of his life, as he spent his entire life doing, as he put it, "some little thing in the spirit of Jesus."

The symbol of Jesus provided the center for a Bonhoeffer, a Tillich, a Teilhard de Chardin; and it provides a center for the most unlettered, humming at evening time *Sweet Little Jesus Boy* . . . even for one whose thinking has never gone beyond "Jesus loves me, this I know."

The symbol of Jesus shows a myriad of contours, shapes and forms; and yet, all provide a center.

Jesus, himself, spoke of inward peace, the center of inward joy, moving him, motivating him, assuring him, giving his life purpose and direction, meaning and significance. His center was balanced and in equilibrium.

For many, the religious center point today is in a process of change and transition, but the search for a center point goes on. We thirst for mystery, for meaning, for community, celebrated through some kind of ritual. We thirst for an unwobbling center point.

For some it will be the Tao, for some the rich heritage of Judaism, for some the tranquility of Zen Buddhism, for some the person of Jesus. But an unwobbling center point there must be, or lives become aimless, and unbalanced.

"At the still point of the turning world . . .
there the dance is . . .
And do not call it fixed . . .
where past and future are gathered . . .
The light is still . . . at the still point . . .
Of the turning world."

Who Are The Christians?

I have always enjoyed the response of John Adams to the clergy of his day when he was accused of not being a "Christian." Founding father Adams told them: "This is my religion, joy and exaltation . . . so go ahead and snarl, bite, howl, all of you Calvinistic divines and you who say I am no Christian. I say you are not 'Christian.' So there, we are even."

I could not help but think of Adams' response last week when an unbelievable book was placed in my hands that described who is and who is not a "Christian." The book was Billy Graham's *Christian Life and Witness Course* given to all of his "counselors" at the crusades (published in 1979).

All of you Mormons out there will be surprised to know that you are not Christians at all, but that you are a "cult" (page 44). Also, on page 41, we find that you Christian Scientists are not Christian, because Billy says that God is a person, and a "male" person at that, and you Christian Scientists do not believe that, and you too are a "cult." Also, you Jehovah's Witnesses are not Christians, either, because you only believe that Jesus was raised as a "divine spirit" (page 43).

Well, enough. The arrogant presumptuousness of such suffocating judgments, as to who is and is not "Christian" leaves me gasping for a breath of fresh air.

Words mean only what we want them to mean. The snake-handler in the hills of the Southeast wrapping rattlesnakes around his neck in a church service calls himself "Christian." Ku Klux Klan members call themselves "Christian." The distinguished theologian-philosopher Paul Tillich called himself a "Christian."

Too many of us forget the symbolic nature of language. Words are only oral or written symbols. We say "the sun rises and sets." Well, any child knows the sun does not "rise" and it does not "set." It is the Earth that is rotating.

I say "a Jew named Jesus." What emotionally charged words those are. There will be as many different emotional and intellectual responses to those symbols as there are people. How we respond to those symbols will depend on our background.

We say "our father in heaven." Many try to read the symbols literally and factually. Does anyone really think that "God" is a "male person" sitting "up" there somewhere behind some cloud? We know there is no such thing as "up" and "down." What is now "up" will shortly be "down," as the Earth rotates.

We say, "Jesus rose from the dead." Do we believe that literally and factually, a body rose from the Earth and like a launched Cape Kennedy missile ascended into the clouds picking up speed and altering heading. If so, where is the body headed? I am talking about the symbolic nature of all language. And religious language is perhaps the most symbolic of all.

The dollar-grabbing evangelist on the Mexican border radio stations knows that by tossing out such emotionally charged symbols as "Jesus Christ" . . . "the blood of the lamb" . . . etc., all stewed together in a real smorgasbord of catch phrases and cliches, the gullible will make him a multimillionaire. And add to this his hawking prayers and pushing four-color reprints of the Last Supper.

Oral Roberts calls a press conference and tells them he saw a 900-foot Jesus who told him he needed more money. He got millions from the gullible. After he ran out of that pile, he called another press conference and said he saw this 900-foot Jesus again and in came more money.

The gullible, who continually bite at emotionally charged religious-word symbols, do not ever seem to realize that a salmon thinks every shiny thing that goes through the water is a minnow and that is why he gets the hook. As the eminent semanticist, S. I. Hayakawa put it: "Understanding the symbolic nature of language can save us from making a fool out of ourselves."

Far too many so-called "Christians" want everyone else to read and interpret the symbols in exactly the same way they do, based on their own narrow frame of reference. And if you do not, they say you are simply not a "Christian," as they go smugly on their way. And so to the presumptuous Calvinistic divines, who assured John Adams he was no Christian, Adams replied: "Well now, I say you are no Christian. So there, we are even." You might remember that response the next time you are told you are not a "real" Christian.

Founding Fathers Would Howl
If Called Christian

In few other areas of American history is there such a distortion of facts as there is regarding the religious orientation of our Founding Fathers.

A recent Guest Opinion columnist wrote in *The Idaho Statesman* that: "200 years ago, having religion meant one's life had been drastically altered by the saving lordship of Jesus Christ. Our country was founded by 'born again' men of heart and mind." Those statements are absurd.

George Washington, Thomas Jefferson, John Adams, James Madison, Benjamin Franklin (and even Abraham Lincoln, another of our most admired Presidents) must be turning over in their graves and weeping at such a perversion of their beliefs.

Our most distinguished Founding Fathers did *not* believe in a "personal" God . . . they did *not* believe that the Bible was anything other than literature . . . and they had an almost contempt for the Christian clergy and Christian doctrine. "God" was to them "nature's god"; an impersonal form, or "providence." Thomas Paine said it for all of them in these words: "Men and books lie. Only nature does not lie."

In the interest of truth and integrity, I will let these brilliant men speak for themselves:

George Washington refused to ever take communion (looking upon it as superstition), refused to recite liturgy and refused to kneel. Historians classify him as a deist, as did his contemporaries. He never, at any time, professed any "Christian" doctrine or dogma. Episcopalian Bishop Wilson declared Washington to be "only a Unitarian if anything." Historians say that Washington recommended and concurred with American Consul Joel Barlow's statement, written in the Treaty of Peace and Friendship that: "The government of the United States is not in any sense founded on the Christian religion."

John Adams wrote "This is my religion . . . joy and exaltation in my own existence . . . so go ahead and snarl . . . bite . . . howl, you Calvinistic divines and all you who say I am no Christian. I say you are not Christian." Regarding the trinity, he wrote this to Jefferson, "Tom, had you and I been 40 days with Moses, and beheld the great God, and even if God himself had tried to tell us that three was one . . . and one equals three, you and I would never have believed it. We would never fall victims to such lies."

Thomas Jefferson, the sole author of the Declaration of Independence (outside of minor word changes), called the Bible a "dunghill" and said that to remove a few of the teachings of Jesus was to "remove the few diamonds from the dunghill." Other quotes: "Christianity is the most perverted system that ever shone on man" and "The authors of the gospels were unlettered and ignorant men and the teachings of Jesus have come to us mutilated, misstated and unintelligible."

Benjamin Franklin wrote: "I have found Christian dogma unintelligible. Early in life I absented myself from Christian assemblies."

James Madison wrote: "During almost 15 centuries the legal establishment known as Christianity has been on trial, and what have been its fruits, more or less in all places? THESE ARE THE FRUITS: Pride, indolence, ignorance and arrogance in the clergy. Ignorance . . . arrogance and servility in the laity and IN BOTH CLERGY AND LAITY superstition, bigotry, and persecution."

Thomas Paine, who inspired both James Madison and Abraham Lincoln, wrote: "When I see throughout this book, called the Bible, a history of the grossest vices and a collection of the most paltry and contemptible tales and stories, I could not so dishonor my Creator by calling it by His name."

Abraham Lincoln said: "I have never united myself to any church because I could not give assent to the long complicated statements of Christian doctrine and dogma which characterize their articles of belief and confession of faith. When any church will require only the Great Commandment (the Jewish Shema) for belief, then I will join that church." Lincoln would never be baptized . . . he would never make any profession of "Christian" faith . . . he would never affiliate with any church or denomination . . . he never subscribed to any liturgy or ritual. His own wife said, "My husband is not a Christian but is a religious man, I think."

Perhaps the point is made for those who would care to pursue it further prior to making statements that will cause the enlightened to blush with embarrassment.

A show of hands on how many would like our Founding Fathers' religious orientation to have been different is not going to change the facts. In the interest of integrity, let us not be celebrating what never was, for there is much we can celebrate that was. The wells of significant, profound and enriching "religion" ran far deeper in most of these men than in a great many orthodox Christians . . . of both yesterday and today.

Too many of us are like the priests of Gallileo's day who refused to look through the telescope for fear of what they might see. And too many of us are like the lady who, when first told about evolution, responded with, "Well, let us pray to God it is not true, but IF IT IS TRUE, then let us pray to God nobody ever hears about it."

Ancient Texts Define A
Zen Christianity

In 1945 an Arab peasant in the upper Egyptian desert near Nag Hammadi made a spectacular discovery. Buried in earthenware were 52 papyrus texts, some dating from the beginning of the Christian era and presenting a Jesus that said things that could have come out of the mouth of a Zen Master, or even the Buddha himself.

Professor Helmut Koester of Harvard University has made the observation that one of these gospels in particular, the *Gospel of Thomas*, includes traditions even older than the Gospels of *The New Testament*, earlier than *Matthew, Mark, Luke* or *John*. They are known as the Gnostic gospels, from the Greek word gnosis — meaning 'to know,' to know oneself, to have an insight into oneself in an intuitive sense.

"To know oneself is to know God," says Jesus in these gospels. The self and the divine are identical and one. The living Jesus in these gospels speaks of enlightenment, the same type that is taught by Zen Masters and Taoists. Jesus is never presented as Lord, but rather as a spiritual guide. The living Buddha could easily have said, and did, everything attributed to Jesus in the *Gospel of Thomas* and other of the texts.

These texts, with Jesus talking in this manner, were seen as a danger to the developing ecclesiastical structure because they encouraged insubordination to the authority of bishops, priests and deacons. Church father Ignatius warns the laity to "honor and obey the bishop as you would God."

He continues, "For the Bishop presides in the place of God." It is quite easy to see why the church councils did not choose these gospels for their Bible. It was purely political. Bishops and priests "can't get no respect" from the common people, if the common people read that Jesus said they don't need bishops and priests and that "the Kingdom is all within everyone, and all are sons of God."

Jesus says in the *Gospel of Thomas:* "If you bring forth what is within you, what you bring forth will save you . . . for the lamp of the body is the mind." And again, "The mind is the guide, but reason is the teacher. Live according to your mind. Acquire strength for the mind is strong. Enlighten your mind . . . light the lamp within you."

In the *Gospel of Thomas*, Jesus also ridicules those who think of the "Kingdom of God" in literal terms (as if it were a specific, actual place). Jesus says these words, "If those who lead you say to you, 'Look, the Kingdom is in the sky,' then the birds will arrive there before you do. If they say to you you, 'Look, it is in the sea,' then the fish will arrive before you. Instead . . . the Kingdom is a state of self discovery. The Kingdom is inside of you and outside of you. When you come to know yourself, you will know that YOU are the Son of God, but if you do not learn this, you will live in poverty."

His disciples said to Jesus, "When will the Kingdom come?" Jesus replied, "Do you not understand, what you look forward to has already come . . . but you do not recognize it. The Kingdom of heaven is spread out upon the Earth . . . now . . . and men do not see it." The Kingdom is a state of transformed consciousness. The creation and God are one. Humans (man) and God are one.

Jesus said in the *Gospel of Thomas,* "Split wood; I am there. Lift up the stone and you will find me there." Jesus, in these gospels, insists again and again on the primacy of immediate experience as a guide to truth. No one else can tell another which way to go, what to do, how to act or what path to follow. "When you become mature," said Jesus, "you will no longer rely on outside human testimony." This thought, expressed by Jesus in these gospels, is at the heart of Buddhism and Taoism.

There are many scholars and other clergy today within Christianity that are synthesizing the great themes found in the Eastern religions with the sayings of a Jesus that was, quite obviously, far more oriented toward their view of life and reality than we have been led to believe. Paul Tillich, the great Protestant Christian theologian at Harvard and the University of Chicago, wrote a number of brilliant books on this same subject.

And for those of you who want to pursue it further, a Roman Catholic Jesuit, William Johnson, in his book, *Silent Music,* writes of this subject. This Jesuit priest has been studying with Zen Masters for years in Japan, integrating these great themes. He writes of the time that truth broke through to him about the nature of reality, the reality of the oneness of everything, including the oneness of God and man.

When that jar was smashed at Nag Hammadi, that Arab peasant could not have dreamed what far-reaching implications his discovery would have. As Dr. James Robinson of the Institute of Antiquity and Christianity put it: "The entire history of the origins of Christianity, including the life of Jesus, are going to have to be rewritten." These 52 scrolls have unlocked a Zen Jesus and a Zen Christianity.

THE SHIVA

Julie picked up a piece of wood in her yard one day and saw the diety Shiva. Without saying anything about her interpretation, she asked me: 'what do you see?' 'The dancing Shiva', I answered, and so it became a part of her art work.

Shiva symbolizes the cosmic dance of creation and the overcoming of the demonic forces of destruction. There is only the dance, the dance of life. Atoms and porpoise dance, aspen leaves and willow boughs dance, hawks dance with the wind and hummingbirds dance around the flower. It is a cosmic dance of creation and joy.

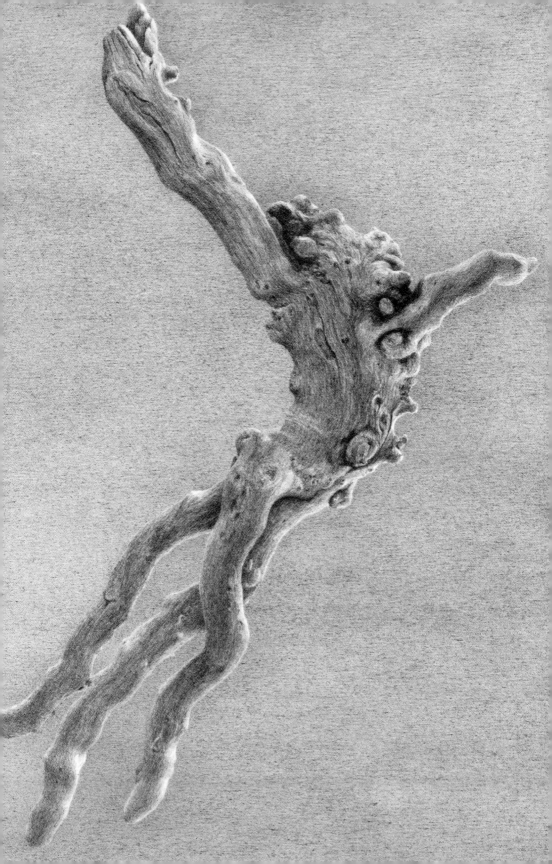

THE HOLIDAY SEASONS

"The most beautiful thing we can underline{experience} is the underline{mysterious}. It is the source of all TRUE ART AND SCIENCE."
— *Albert Einstein*

"God does not die on the day when we cease to believe in a personal deity, but we die on the day when our lives cease to be illumined by the steady radiance . . . renewed daily . . . of a wonder . . . the source of which is beyond all reason."
— *Dag Hammarskjold*

" . . . 'words' occupy an ambiguous status in life. 'Words' build up a substitute world that dilutes the intensity of direct spontaneous experience. The highest modes of 'experience' completely transcend the reach of any language."
— *the position of Zen Buddhism*

"By what right do we take this little agitation of the brain, which we call 'thought' . . . by what right do we finite mortals . . . arrogate to ourselves the ability to comprehend the infinite mystery . . . we call God?"
— *the philosopher Hume*

Thanksgiving Reminds Us How Goodness Outweighs Evil

I am sitting here at my typewriter thinking about Thanksgiving day next week. I am wondering what it would be like to just let my fingers start typing a letter to God. Yes, I like that.

As usual, I will begin with "Dear." "Dear . . ." what? I realize that I am in trouble already. Dear Sir? Dear Madam? Dear Ms.? Dear It? Dear First Principle? Dear Cosmic Energy? Dear Truth? Dear Love? Well, Whatever and Whomever, here it is:

Thanksgiving week again, and I am supposed to remember all of those things I am thankful for. The nice and good things no doubt. But how about all of those things not so nice and good. What about those? When I lived in the Pacific Northwest, I used to go out sometimes in my bare feet, in the dark, to get the morning paper. Now I am asking you, God, do you know what it is like to be walking, barefoot, on the drive and step on a slug? Have you ever stepped on a slug in bare feet? How could you have made slugs?

I am thinking too of bigger mistakes than slugs. What was your point in cancer, earthquakes and tornadoes? Or how about insanity and war, starvation and Hitler? We say arson is a crime, and yet your "laws" are continually allowing arson through forest fire, lightning and volcano.

We say poisoning is a crime, but your "laws" continually poison us with cobra, rattlesnake, cottonmouth and viper. Your "laws" are continually doing things that we execute people for down here on Earth.

And now, on Thanksgiving, I am supposed to sing "praises" as to how "good" you are and be grateful. I am remembering a line from the Pulitzer Prize-winning play *J. B.* by Archibald MacLeish: "If god is God, He is not good; if god is good, he is not God, take the even, take the odd."

Well God, you know I have to be fair. If I am stumped before the mystery of evil, I am also stumped before the mystery of goodness and beauty. And there *is goodness,* beauty and love, such as: sunrises over Jughandle mountain at McCall . . . music and symphonies and the laughter of children and adults at play . . . magnificent books and art . . . literature and breath-taking science . . . aspen, painting the mountains with strokes of yellow, amber and gold . . . frost, sparkling at first light . . . and where would it end, remembering the beauty?

Sure, there have been Hitlers; but I remember Jesus . . . and also Goethe, Shakespeare, Handel, Schweitzer, Jung, Helen Keller, Galileo, Copernicus, Gandhi, Buddha and all of those millions and millions of kind, wonderful and gentle folk whose names are not known half a mile from home.

I am still thankful for the Bachs and the Beethovens. When I have seen a child born blind, I have cried, "What evil." But then I remember Helen Keller, who upon receiving her honorary degree at the University of Glasgow, reminded us: "It is a sign that darkness and silence need not bar the progress of the immortal spirit."

Well, do you know what, God? With all of these things on my mind, I can still say I have no idea who and what you are. It always bothers me terribly to hear ministers and others try to explain you. They cannot even explain a light bulb, and yet they will dive right in telling everyone all about you . . . and how you operate your thousands of galaxies and light year spaces. And then, when they start telling people here on this little speck called Earth what you want them to do and what books you don't like, and what movies bother you, well, I am sure you must find it all very comical, especially when some football team thanks you for allowing them to carry a pig hide across a chalk line more often than the other team. You, the author of billions upon billions of planets, galaxies and timeless "space."

Saying that I have no idea who and what you are . . . is the origin of my faith. It seems to me that trusting in something behind this cosmos that I cannot conceive of is a much higher and sustaining form of faith than if I fervently, desperately, clung to some mental conception of you, some idol created in my own mind.

Faith, to me, begins with the conviction that the basic elements in the cosmos are good. Faith is a feeling that deep at the heart of this universe is a Spirit not ourselves . . . and from this Spirit come "laws" that never slip, so unified that if I lift my finger the farthest galaxy feels the impulse . . . and from this Spirit come trees and human souls . . . stars and galaxies and human minds . . . and from this Spirit come human spirits that rise above apparent evil and overcome it.

I remember that Jesus never said: "I have explained the world." He just said, "I have overcome it."

It seems to me, God, that faith is not any neat, finished and crystallized creed or "belief," but rather it is betting my life on the constructive forces of truth in this universe — against all those forces that seem to be evil.

Well, God, that's about it. How thankful I am for all the good . . . the beauty . . . the love . . . the hope . . . the faith that has been released into this world and into my life. I don't need to try and explain it. It needs no translation, even as the sound of rain needs no translation. It just is. For I remember there are more magnificent sunsets over the Olympic Mountains, and more flowers than there are tornadoes.

There are more apples, peaches and pears than there are forest fires and volcanoes.

There are more robins, bluebirds, cardinals, hummingbirds and thrushes than there are slugs.

And I think far, far more good than there is evil.

Whoever you are, and wherever, I say faith is not worrying about having to explain you, justify you, defend you or define you.

Faith is knowing that wherever the good, the true and the beautiful touches me, we have met . . . you and I.

And I have experienced who you are. Knowing that, I can sing with feeling on this Thanksgiving day, as one of your children of the universe — and as one of your thankful people.

Much love,
One of your sons,
Bill.

"Did the Almighty, holding in his right hand TRUTH, and in his left hand SEARCH AFTER TRUTH, deign to tender me the one I might prefer, in all humility, but WITHOUT HESITATION, I should request SEARCH AFTER TRUTH."

– Gotthold Lessing

"Time makes ancient good uncouth . . .
They must upward still and onward . . .
Who would KEEP ABREAST of TRUTH."

– from the hymn "Once to Every
Man and Nation"

We Owe Our Thanks To Brave Pioneers

In the book of Deuteronomy is a pungent reminder for this Thanksgiving season: "You drink here from cisterns that you did not dig . . . and you live in cities that you did not build . . . and you eat from vineyards and orchards that you did not plant."

Last week, I was again thinking of our Western pioneers, and I became overwhelmed at our indebtedness to these magnificent and hardy people. I am so proud of our pioneer heritage and of our people. I am remembering in this season the debt we owe to their quest, their dreams and their vision. And I remember . . .

I remembered that in the 1800s the great plains were bare and windswept. There was the wind, the heat, the cold and the unbelievable hardship. But the broad valley of the Platte River and the Columbia called to men and women to come to this country and make a home.

After the mountain men had passed through, and the trappers had migrated to the Western mountains, the prairie schooners came in to settle the land. Along the valley of the Platte they came. There was the Platte River, running muddy from the feet of more buffalo than the eye could count. It was, they said, a mile wide and a foot deep.

Along the Platte they came with their flour, quilts, bacon, dried stuff, meal, coffee and a little keg of vinegar. Names were on their lips — names such as Red Cloud, Sitting Bull, Crazy Horse, Cheyenne, Arapaho, Sioux, Nez Perce, Blackfoot and Shoshone.

On they came with dry, hot winds, grasshoppers and drought, sickness and disease, blizzard and hail. And they stayed and built a land.

They dug stumps and planted fields. They dug cisterns and planted orchards and vineyards. They built one room schools and churches. They started a town. They had babies and more babies. They raised families and worshiped God.

Their children played with dust swirl, horned toads and tumbleweed. They played at the edge of rushing river and mountain stream. They played in forest glade and alpine meadow. And they grew. They grew as hardy and as courageous, as brave and as visionary as the parents who gave them birth.

And so today, you and I, we "drink from cisterns that we did not dig, and we live in cities that we did not build, and we eat from vineyards and orchards that we did not plant."

In this Thanksgiving season I am remembering the debt that we owe to those magnificent people, the debt on which no payments have been demanded. There are times when I am ashamed of my acceptance of myriad contributions without a thought of those who gave them.

How little time we spend, remembering with gratitude and

thanksgiving, all that we owe to others who have contributed to our growth and existence. Lest pride kill our memory, let us remember those who have helped us and encouraged us along the way. We can remember that no child can ever repay the debt they owe to wise and loving and caring parents.

Do you not remember the teacher who opened your eyes and enlarged your vision and exposed you to worlds of knowledge that you never even knew existed? How well I remember such teachers in this Thanksgiving season with a gratitude that is beyond measure. The only way we can possibly repay the debt we owe them is by passing it on to others.

How thankful I am for the great thinkers of civilization and all of the great ideas that have enriched my life and fed my spirit.

All of these blessings that flow into our lives, from the mystery that sustains our days and the beat of our heart, to those we receive from one another, we can call . . . grace.

In this Thanksgiving season we can never repay all of the debts that we owe for there are so many.

We can only respond in gratitude and gratefulness to this . . . grace . . . that we have received by passing it on to our neighbor.

We swallow our pride. We open our hard hearts. We realize our debts, and we say "thank you" to many for all of the graces that have been so freely given.

In gratitude we say to our neighbor . . . grace . . . peace.

And a silent voice "overheard by the soul" comes to us, saying, "grace, and peace to you."

Legend, Fantasy Wrap Many Spiritual Traditions

Biologists may classify us as Homo sapiens, "the wise one," but I would also note that we are Homo storialus — the animal who tells stories.

We tell them through folklore, legend and myth, and then act them out in ritual. It is safe to say that stories plus ritual equal religion. Stories are the threads by which we weave the tapestry of our culture, our religions and our traditions.

The literalistic skeptic says: "I don't want legends, I want FACTS." He does not understand the observation made by D. H. Lawrence that there are TWO kinds of truth — a truth of *facts* and a truth of *truth*. A truth of facts has to do with dates, places and so forth. But the truth of truth is revealed to us through myth, legend, folklore, fairy tales and has to do with the inner world of the imagination and emotions. They reveal the inner shape and contour of our minds, our longings and needs, our spirits.

Even though we have long forgotten what original question a story answered, it is in our heritage and repeated year after year, through story and ritual. We are now entering a beautiful, lovely period of folklore, legend and fantasy.

"We Three Kings of Orient Are" is a perfect example. First, no one has any idea how many wise men there were. There could have been two or 50. Second, they were not kings, and third, they did not come from as far away as the Orient. Folklore decided on the number three. They were magicians and came from no further away than Persia. The magicians were not Hebrew and would have been considered pagans. At any rate, through folklore, they and their three camels are with us every Christmas to help celebrate this wonderful time.

On New Year's, we will kiss under the mistletoe. How many remember that the origin of this goes back to the Druids? Mistletoe was a sacred plant, equal to the sacredness of the sun. They went in solemn procesion for the annual cutting on the sixth day of the moon nearest the New Year. A priest officiated clad in white robes and bearing a golden knife. Any maid who went unkissed under the mistletoe on the oak trees went without a husband for another year. This legend is absorbed in our Christian customs and is still practiced as a lovely ritual, a relic from an old, old religion and an old, old story.

We sing carols. Now we call them Christmas carols, forgetting the folk song origin of many of them, or that the midwinter observance of Saturn in Rome was celebrated with joyful carols and that, long before the birth of Jesus, candles were used at the same time in Rome to light young pine trees.

Or that holly was used for festival decorations for centuries before Jesus. Legend says that holly kept away witches and brought charm wherever it was used.

Or we forget that long before the birth of Jesus, Egyptians worshipped before statues of the virgin mother, Isis, suckling her child, Horus, who was miraculously conceived in a stable. Early Christians, for years, worshipped before similar statues . . . of Isis suckling her divine child, Horus. And everyone knows that the date, December 25, is in no way the factual, actual date of Jesus' birth.

The Christmas tree has been traced back in mythology, almost to the paleolithic period.

There are many who think it terribly disrespectful to write Christmas with an X as X-mas. What they forget is the X-mas is an ancient word, coming to us from the Greek language. "X" was the symbol for the word, "Christ," and so today is still practiced, with no disrespect.

Let's look at the New Year's celebration. All the noise and clamor are only a vestige of the myth of the eternal rhythms and the eternal return, the periodic destruction and recreation of the cosmos, common to all religions: a time when the world and man, after a ritual pause, became ritually renewed.

A child asks: "When does the *old* year end?"

"On the first stroke of midnight," answers Mary Poppins.

"And the *new* year, when does it begin?" asks the child.

"On the last stroke of midnight," says Mary Poppins.

"Well then," asks the child, "what happens in between while the clock is striking 12?"

The child has naturally, once again, stumbled upon the question, celebrated for centuries in primitve religions (as well as others) of the ritual pause.

Stories, legends and folklore are the raw materials of our spiritual life and our traditions. Where would they end?

There are many in our society who want us to live without myth, without fantasy and legend. What they would substitute is technology, science and ideologies as a means of discovering meaning and celebrating values. They would have us live by abstractions, rules and laws rather than by stories that tell of things past . . . and images of the future.

But we are still story-telling animals, who annually celebrate the stories that enrich our lives and the inner world of our emotions and our souls. The brilliant George Santayana, former chairman of the Department of Philosophy at Harvard University, wrote that "long after I had rejected, intellectually, institutional Christianity, I still returned every Christmas Eve for the beauty and the significance of the candlelight Mass. It fed my soul and my spirit."

We still hunger for a story that will in some way dramatize a meaning to existence that we can hold to. We still need a story that begins "once upon a time."

"Coming home" still sleeps in our breast and gives significance to our days and to our inner world. It is in this inner world where we take the threads of stories and weave the tapestry of our own life and the world we live in . . . a world that is our very own truth of truth.

"How wondrously supernatural, spiritual and miraculous this: fetching water and chopping wood."
– Zen

"Seeking God is like riding on an ox looking for an ox to ride."
– Taoism

"The eye by which I see God is the same as the eye by which God sees me. My eye and God's eye are one and the same."
– Meister Eckhart (Christian)

"One who tries to divide life between a relation with God and a relation with the world is the truly GODLESS PERSON . . . NOT the atheist."
– Martin Buber

Which Road Will You Take
This Christmas?

We go out the great south gate of Jerusalem, over the rolling Judean hills, down the dusty road past Rachel's white-domed tomb, to the city of David.

It isn't really far — past the wise men's well, past shepherds with reed flutes, past boys playing on the hillside slopes — and soon we are there, looking down on the dazzling, sun-white roofs of Bethlehem.

As we approach this special time of the year, we know that we must set our minds and our hearts toward this Oriental city (whether or not we even really want to). The press and advertising of the world will carry us to this scene of Jesus' birth. The world will have its Christmas. So the question is not: "Are we going to Bethlehem?" The question is: "Which road are we going to take?"

For there are two roads that lead to this city of David, and they are as different as can be. What we gain from this Christmas season depends on the road that we choose.

Stretching arrow straight from Jerusalen south to Bethlehem is the first road — broad, smooth and wide. It is a joy to our eyes and a tempting invitation to our feet, for this is a proud example of the road-building art perfected by the Roman Empire.

Perhaps the strongest inducement for us to take this first road to Bethlehem is the holiday-spirited crowd that will become our companions. These carefree men and women are out on a holiday. They know why they are heading for Bethlehem. There will be parties there and a veneer-like gaiety will be everywhere. For a few brief days, these people on this first road can escape from the boredom of their lives, using this time as an excuse for excesses of every kind. Revelry will reign king.

Do you recognize this first road to Bethlehem? Have you not seen the invitation sprinkled through your magazines, newspapers and hanging in gay red and green letters from counters and assaulting our homes from our television screens?

The invitation to this first road reads: "Come to Christmas with the department stores and the gift decanters. Christmas is on sale again this year."

This highway to Bethlehem is filled with people already, through all the shopping days left until Christmas.

We are all, in some way, going to be a part of the crowd on the first road. All I am saying is: Let's keep this first road in perspective. It is good to gather together in lovely and gracious parties; it is good and beautiful to gather around trees and give and receive gifts of love and affection; it is good to celebrate with loved ones and laugh and play and know joy and happiness.

This can be a season of beauty, if perspective is maintained, and if the second road is not forgotton. And there is a second road.

This second road was there centuries before the first Roman road was started. Millions of simple folk have worn its clay surface smooth. This road is not the easiest or the quickest to Bethlehem. The road is not straight or smooth.

We can recognize some of our traveling companions on this narrow path. There is an anxious husband carefully leading the donkey on which his wife, already great with child, is seated. There are scurrying shepherd boys. Later, there will be strange scholars from the East, consulting their ancient parchments and glancing heavenward every few moments to be sure they are on the right road.

We shall have to keep in perspective the clear, steady call from those on the other wide road. We have to forget for a time the "special holiday decanter" and "only 13 shopping days left."

We have to forget the blaring noise coming from the other road and go away from the city and lights to join those keeping watch over their flocks by night, and with them search the sky for a Christmas comet or an Eastern star.

Only on this road will we have time to be alone with our thoughts and prepare our hearts for what we are truly seeking.

Two roads lead into Bethlehem, but only one continues now. The first broad, Roman road ends abruptly and comes to an end on December 26. The revelry is over. But the narrow road leads on past the stable, out of Bethelehem to Galilee, through all Palestine witnessing to a new hope and new life.

Bethlehem awaits us. The choice is ours. With no effort we can drift along with the crowd prepared to snatch, with fleeting pleasure, what we may find. Or, we can take the slower, but more meaningful road, making it a time of introspection, a time for new insights.

"And so I shall be telling this with a sigh somewhere ages and ages hence. Two roads diverged, and I . . . I chose the one less traveled by . . . and that has made all the difference."

Make Room For Season's Truth And Joy

As Luke paints the birth picture of Jesus, he uses these words, "There was *no room* for them in the inn." It was almost like prophecy, was it not? That was pretty much to be the story of his life . . . no room for his teachings . . . no room for his spirit . . . no room for him in the hearts and minds he longed to change.

Is that not the story of too many lives? There is no room for those things that are excellent . . . no room for the lovely and the beautiful . . . no room for truth. Great books are not read . . . great music is not listened to. In our proccupation with trivia, the highest is shut out.

There are beauties in nature to be experienced, but we are too busy. We miss enriching friendships and human relationships . . . and the possibilities of genuine joy . . . because we are too busy. There is no room . . . we are too preoccupied.

We have no time to sit down and meditate upon the great and majestic religious writings of man at his most inspired and creative moments. We have no time to ponder and meditate upon magnificent truths that are available for only a few dollars in any good bookstore.

In this season we might reflect upon the truth — that which we find room for, and what we say "yes" to, is about as important and self-revealing an act as any we perform. We find room for the things we really care about, the things that are important to us.

Individually and collectively, our own growth, enlightenment, enlargement, and developing is directly related to how much of truth, love and beauty coming our way actually finds room in our minds and hearts. Next to being creative and great yourself is the ability to recognize greatness when you see it . . . and then make room for it. To be able to recognize greatness, and then listen to it, is one of the truly great gifts.

There are some in this season who pride themselves on being analytical of mind, and who look upon all this Christmas business with shrewd, appraising eyes. If that is all we do, it can totally impoverish and stunt out lives.

For instance, I have many times stood on the banks of Jenny Lake in the Grand Tetons of Wyoming, from the pre-dawn to sunset hours, and gazed across that crystal clear, placid lake to the opposite shore where the Grand Teton rises, soaring almost vertically to over 10,000 feet, and guarded on each side by the other two slightly lesser peaks. Tumblng down into Jenny Lake, gently brushing the base of the Teton and making a joyful noise, is the water whose origin was the snows above Lake Solitude, high in the high country where I have often hiked.

Now an analyst is quite correct in saying that this lake, this water, is nothing more than two parts of hydrogen to one part of oxygen. That is an important truth. And this oxygen and hydrogen, combined, is merely obeying the law of gravity as it pushes igneous rocks out of the way — or goes around them. That's all true. An analyst is quite correct in saying that these Tetons are granite — igneous rocks — consisting chiefly of crystalline quartz, mica and feldspar. This is quite correct, and that is a part of truth.

But to stop there is to impoverish my life. Something else is really, genuinely there . . . and *is truth* and is more than analysis. That something else is of my heart, my emotions, my mind, my spirit, my soul.

It has to do with reflections, receptivity, appreciation, insight, responsiveness, a sensitivity to form and texture and color, a sensitivity to beauty, a sensitivity to feeling, a sensitivity to truth, that has often left me breathless. There have been times when the beauty of that scene has moved me to gentle tears.

That is truth, too, equally as great, and maybe even a higher truth than that having to do with hydrogen and oxygen and igneous rocks. For the truth that can move to tears has to do with the spirit.

I know that December 25 was not the literal birthday of Jesus, even as I know that Jenny Lake is only hydrogen and oxygen.

I know that "virgin birth" was a common theme, motif, or formula found in many religions indicating divine significance. Ishtar in Babylon was called the virgin mother; Isis in Egypt was called the virgin mother of Horus, immaculately conceived; Lao Tzu, the old master of Taoism was said to have been born of a virgin, sired by a star from the East; Zoroaster was said to have been born of a virgin; and Buddhists tell that at the divine birth of Buddha, the entire cosmos was flooded with a brilliant light and all evil spirits fled. The blind could see. The lame could walk. The deaf could hear and the dumb could speak. I know those truths even as I know that the Tetons are only igneous rock. That is a truth.

But the higher truth . . . that speaks to my spirit . . . is the spirit of the occasion, the spirit of the celebration, the spirit of the presence that recalls to my attention the nature of love and the nature of truth.

When I make room for that presence — and all that presence represented, taught, and revealed — something happens to me, something that is what Christmas is all about. And that is the highest truth.

How much of the best and most beautiful that is a part of you and me, is measured only by how much of it we have made room for?

Good things of great joy shall always be with us . . . *if we make room.*

Gift Of Kindness Brightens Lives Around You

As we prepare to enter the beauty of this Christmas season, let our thoughts and reflections be upon the "art" of kindness. One of the classic works of Erich Fromm was a little book entitled *The Art of Loving*. His thesis was that "love" is an art to be learned. We are not born with it. So it is with kindness.

Kindness is an art to be cultivated. It begins in the home. It is learned by the way father and mother treat each other, and the way both of them treat their children. But even if we are so unfortunate as to have come from a home where kindness was unknown, it is no excuse. It is never too late to start learning kindness, whether we are 10 or 85.

Where do we start? We start with our imagination. You "imagine" yourself as being that other person that you are about to dive into. Project yourself into that other life, mentally. Surely you are not so drugged with self-obsession, self-centeredness and self-preoccupation that you cannot do this.

You have just walked into the department store, spotted a saleswoman, and approached her. My heavens, the rudeness of this woman. You cannot believe it. The indifference. Why don't they fire her? Well now, move over across the counter and, in your *imagination*, take her place.

Do you know what happened to her at home this morning before she came to work? Do you know that maybe her child is seriously ill? Bills are piling up. Her husband humiliated her this morning at breakfast in front of the children. Are you aware that all of those things might be on the mind of that saleswoman as she is trying to wait upon you?

You don't like the choir music in your church? All right, *imagine* now that you are the choir director and you are given the responsibility for planning music for the next 48 weeks, plus weddings and funerals added to special programs. You do it in your imagination.

You don't like the sermons. That's understandable. I do some I don't like either. OK, now, you've got it ... the responsibility of producing 48 addresses, 20 to 30 minutes, and keeping them varied, inspirational, enlightening, educational, intellectually honest and academically sound. And they must please everyone. You do it, now, in your imagination.

Kindness grows with practice, and it all begins in your imagination and your ability to listen. You know as well as I that we all, every last one of us, have need for being far more kind than we are.

This does not mean there is not a place for intelligent and sensitive criticism. But it does mean that we very carefully examine the motivation for the critique, the context of it, the validity and the manner in which it is done.

We cultivate kindness just as we cultivate a sense of beauty, or an appreciation for art, or music and literature. It takes practice and effort, make no mistake about it. And gradually we will find our life flowing easily, effortlessly, kindly and lovingly into other lives. Maybe what we need is a miracle of the heart.

Jesus kept insisting that true religion begins in the heart and flows outward. This is the reason for his stern criticism of the Pharisees. Their hearts were hard and cold. They just judged and judged, condemned and condemned. Jesus was critical of the cruelty, the insensitivity and callousness of the Pharisees.

The kindness, the sympathy and the empathy comes through time and time again as Jesus met people along the way. The woman in the house of Simon — how Simon wanted to embarrass and humiliate this woman, which he proceeded to do in a very unkind way. The words of Jesus to the woman were so beautifully kind and loving. The words of Jesus to Simon asked how he could be so heartless and cruel.

In the home of Mary and Martha, after Jesus had finished dinner, Mary took valuable perfume and washed the feet of Jesus. Judas condemned her at once for such waste. Jesus said, "Let her alone. She has done a beautiful thing." Jesus looked at what was in her kind and loving heart. He also saw the hard heart of Judas.

Now Judas may have been right. It may have been a waste, and it might have been wiser to sell the perfume and give the proceeds to the poor . . . it might have been right. But do you realize that a person can be just as right as right can be, and still be as mean, selfish, cruel, unkind and sadistic as any child of hell. I think that I would rather be a kind and loving person, and be WRONG, than be a cruel and unkind person and be right, if I were given the choice.

What is the finest gift you can give your child? Prominence? Never. Wealth? Never. A fine education? Maybe.

Is not the finest gift a knowledge of what it is to live with a great, kind and loving heart? It is an art to be learned. We teach it, "As in filling a vessel drop by drop, there is a last drop which makes the vessel run over. So with kindness, in a series of kindnesses, there is at last one which makes the heart run over."

Let us think and reflect upon these things as we enter the Christmas season, celebrating the life of one who gave us an example . . . of the kind, warm and loving heart.

Christmas Means "God Is Love"

For thousands of years this has been the most special time of the year and the most important date in human celebration, for the sun has started its long journey home bringing with it spring and summer.

Celebrating this event today, you and I are part of a line of descent that has been uninterrupted almost from the birth of humankind.

There has been no time when someone, somewhere, was not celebrating this date. Long before the birth of Jesus our bloodstream ran in the veins of sun gods and sun worshippers: Greeks and Romans . . . Barbarians in the Germanic forests . . . Northern worshippers of Thor . . . Egyptians . . . Jews . . . Gauls, Persians and Indians.

No wonder human beings have celebrated the date of the winter solstice for thousands of years, considering that our very survival depends upon the return of the sun.

No wonder that Julius, the fourth century Pope, when asked to fix a date for the birth of Jesus, said, "we will say it took place in Bethlehem on December 25." It was the date of the winter solstice according to the Julian calendar. The new Christians had already absorbed pagan traditions and customs and so now they could all celebrate together. And so for thousands of years we have celebrated this date with singing and dancing, with solemn ceremony and flowers, palms, mistletoe and holly, plays and majestic processionals moving through high cathedrals. Christmas is in our bloodstream . . . it is in our genes.

Last night, at our beautiful candlelight service, I knew how much was legend, folklore, cultural custom and ritual. I would not deny that. And yet I, once again, experienced the wonder and awe as I faced the great and wonderful mystery. Wonder is astonishment at something awesomely mysterious. Wonder is, perhaps, the ultimate religious attitude. There is little difference between wonder and experiencing the holy. "The sense of wonder . . . is our sixth sense," wrote D. H. Lawrence, "and it is the natural sense."

Wonder is the capacity for sustained and continued delight, marvel, amazement and joy. Wonder is a sense of freshness, anticipation, spontaneity and openness.

"What is our chief end?" asks the Westminster catechism. The answer: "To enjoy God." To enjoy is an attitude of wonder. Whether it be discovering a new flower . . . a butterfly on the breeze . . . a new taste in the kitchen . . . geese honking, silhouetted against a full moon . . . a hug from someone loved . . . a fir tree all covered with bright and shiny things and pretty packages underneath . . . the story of a baby, a stable and a star.

I am filled with wonder at the mystery of the recurring theme of a child, a vision, a star and a revelation. Stars have been a symbol for thousands of years of the eternal God. There was the Bushman, who on a star filled night would hold his new child up high in his arms, pointing toward the stars, saying: "give this child the heart of a star." There was Plato, who said that the stars in the sky are the purest embodiment of the divine nature of reality. There was the philosopher Immanuel Kant, who said "two things fill my mind with awe, the stars in the heavens above me, and the love I feel within me." And, when Jesus was born, wise men from the East came, saying "we have seen his star in the East, and have come to worship."

Do you know what it means to be purely rational? It means that you want to explain everything, and you cannot. We impoverish our life when we try. It is one of the major diseases of our time in the overly scientific, computerized world. Albert Einstein used these words: "The most beautiful thing that we can experience is the mysterious. It is the source of all true art and science. He who cannot feel the mysterious is dead. His eyes and heart are closed."

How many in this glorious season of wonder have ceased to feel the mystery and the symbolism of the event?

Christmas, regardless of how the date was established, asks us to open our eyes and hearts to the wonder of God. No computer will ever explain it, for it is an affair of the heart. What a blessing that Christmas comes each year to enchant us with the story of a star, a birth and a stable. It fills our hearts with hope, with joy and with love. Every new revelation is a gift to those whose hearts can respond with wonder. "How silently, how silently, the wondrous gift is given."

A few years before he died, the brilliant theologian philosopher Paul Tillich said that all of his massive writings in the field of theology could be reduced to a doctrine of only three words: God is love. All the rest, he wrote, can easily be forgotten. To think on that, to understand that and live by it is to be genuinely reborn in this day of birth.

We need no new thoughts for this Christmas day. We need only to remember and live an old thought, that a birth of 2,000 years ago reminds us annually that God is love. It is within our hearts that this spirit must be born new. It is an inner birth possible for you and for me in the continuing miracle of this holy season.

There are, from time to time, mornings when the world begins anew and beyond which memory need not go. These are mornings of creation. These are mornings when the world is recreated. These are mornings when we have been blessed and graced with new life and new hope.

May we all, on this day, know the reality of such a new morning . . . that should follow last . . . silent night . . . holy night . . . where all was calm and all was bright . . . where glories were streaming from heaven afar . . . and we slept . . . in heavenly peace.

I wish, for you and your house, all grace, all joy and all peace on this Christmas day now . . . and forever.

How Christmas Joy Warmed
A Frigid War Scene

Several years ago I was asked by the Tacoma, Washington, *News Tribune* to be on a panel of three judges in their "My Most Memorable Christmas" essay contest.

I thought back over all of my Christmases, and I asked myself, "What year was MY most memorable Christmas? If I could enter the contest, what would I write about?" There was no question. One Christmas stood our brilliantly and flooded back into my mind with memories. That was Christmas in Korea in 1951 . . . what a profound effect it had upon my life.

I cannot tell you what a joy it is to allow all of those thoughts and experiences to flood back into my mind . . . and to write them down to share with you in this season. I was there again flying as an aircraft commander of a Marine Corps transport plane, a DC-3 — the "gooney bird," as we called it.

We had the responsibility of flying wounded evacuation. One of the most famous evacuation sites was a river bottom of hard-packed sand, called Inje. We would fly up the canyon, often only a hundred feet or so above the river, land on the hard-packed sand, pick up the wounded, turn the plane around, and take off again. There was life and death in the more tragic dimensions.

The armies of North Korea were pushing south as if they were a mighty tidal wave, sweeping everything before it, including South Korean armies and civilians. The major southern city was Pusan at the tip of South Korea.

During this mass migration south, it was estimated the population of Pusan increased 10 to 12 times. Can you imagine Boise increasing 10 to 12 times within a 30- to 60-day period? People were "existing" in cardboard box shacks, scraps of wood, clothing — whatever they could find to protect them from the weather.

During this migration, childen were abandoned for many reasons: Either their parents were killed, they became lost, or they were deserted due to the desperation of the mother, father, or relative who was barely surviving. And, for that reason, it was estimated that there were about 9,000 starving, freezing, lost children in the Pusan area . . . with no family, no one they knew, no relatives.

It is cold in the winter in Korea — temperatures of zero and sub-zero. You would see the children going through garbage cans like rats. You would drive your Jeep down the road (all cuddled up in a nice Marine Corps down coat), and you would look in the ditches at the side of the road and see bodies, frozen bodies. They could be 3 years old, 10 years old. You would pass them still alive, walking barefoot . . . a gunny sack for dress or coat, or shirt . . . bones showing . . . skin purple. You could become calloused to it. Many allowed themselves to so become.

It was impossible to get the children in the ditches out of my mind. Christmas was not too far off. It was cold. I wrote a two-page letter to the church I had grown up in, St. Luke's Methodist Church in downtown Oklahoma City, outlining the plight of the children. My letter was passed on later to the *Oklahoma City Times*, which ran the story. The minister of St. Luke's used the letter as the text for a sermon. In the letter I asked for clothing and money . . . money to be sent to the Navy chaplain so that it could be officially accounted for . . . for clothing to be sent to me so I could start distributing it in those places where it would seem to do the most good.

Well, bless St. Luke's and others in Oklahoma City. They responded with several tons of clothing and about $5,000 in cash (as well as I remember the figure). My, what Christmas presents — all of that clothing. You cannot imagine the faces of those children, the faces of joy and of delight.

Scattered around the countryside would be little one-room shacks; we called them "orphanages." Each little building would have anywhere from 25 to 75 children huddling together to keep warm. We would drive around in our Jeeps taking the boxes of clothing and passing it out among the children.

Now can you picture the scene?

We are in a room. I call it a "room" although, more often than not, you could see daylight through the boards. We are surrounded by children. We are opening a box of clothing . . . *and right on top is a USED MINK COAT,* an old used mink coat from America for a freezing Korean child!

The contrast was beyond all known adjectives. An older Korean girl came forward, maybe 10 or 11 years old, her eyes wide in wonder, staring at this coat, this used mink that was so gorgeous on that winter day . . . beyond fantasy, even, in that young tragic life. And, as she slid her bone-thin arms into that mink and hugged it close around her . . . *tears* rolled down her purple cheeks.

You do not forget a scene like that, ever. It is imprinted on your mind forever. It is burned into your consciousness and into your subconsciousness.

I am sure that you will have no trouble understanding why it was the most memorable and joyful Christmas of my life. There are a few very special keepsakes that we all have that are very dear and very cherished. I will tell you what mine is. On World-Wide Communion Sunday in October 1952, the picture used on the Methodist bulletin and inserts was a picture of a friend and myself standing in the middle of smiling, laughing Korean children, handing out clothing.

We are approaching Christmas, you and I, with a roof over our head and with a full stomach (much too full, 99 percent of the time), warm clothing, and surrounded by human beings who care for us. Believe me, if that was all there was under the tree, just a note reminding us of that, then *that would be more than enough cause for joy.*

"If I have stopped only ONE heart from breaking, I shall not have lived in vain," wrote Emily Dickinson. With gratitude for our own blessings, may our Christmas prayer be that . . . during this season and the coming year . . . our hearts open for that *one other heart* that we might keep from breaking, and this season will not have come — and gone — in vain.

Moon Plays Role In Primal Afterlife Concepts

"On the third day he rose again from the dead" . . . You may think I am quoting the Apostles Creed still recited in so many churches, but actually I am quoting from primal religious liturgies that are referring to the resurrection of the moon after the third night of darkness.

"As the moon dieth and cometh to life again, so we also, having to die, will again rise," declared the Juan Capistrano Indians in ceremonies celebrating the resurrection of the new moon, after three nights of darkness and death. Basically the moon was "she," but in some cases "he."

For more than 100,000 years it has been believed that death had no finality and that there was more.

A boon to archaeologists has been the discovery of graves in the Neanderthal period with both artifacts and flower remains, combined with the sensitivity of the burial.

What phenomenon played a vital part of their imagining a life after death? It was quite simply . . . observing the moon. The sun is always the same. The moon, on the other hand, is born new, grows to maturity, dies and is then resurrected. The period of the new moon, the resurrection of the moon, became one of the most important religious celebrations in many cultures.

Even as late as 600 B.C. in the Hebrew culture of *Old Testament* times, the new moon demanded special and generous offering and sacrifices. Wrote Ezekiel in the *Old Testament*, "On the day of the new moon shall be offered a young bull without blemish and six lambs and a ram which shall be without blemish."

The Hebrew Sabbath was originally a new moon celebration. As the moon is reborn at the end of the third day, so shall the dead be reborn to a new life. Even church father St. Augustine, writing within the framework of 4th century Christianity, still used the cycles of the moon as proof that there was a resurrection from the dead. Little did he dream that someday we would walk on that same moon.

Other beliefs, in such developed countries as India, Greece and Iran, were that the dead went to live on the moon. In India, souls lived on the moon while awaiting reincarnation. In Persia, only the very good went to live on the moon where after a short stay they received the beautiful blessing of being allowed to graduate on toward the infinite light, Mazda. So there developed an almost universal belief based on the cycles of the moon. Death is not final, for the moon's death was not final.

Other beliefs add to life after death concepts. In Egypt, there is a body of religious texts known as the Pyramid texts, dating around 2500 B.C., although they incorporate much older material, describing how the dead shall go before Osiris with their declaration of innocence. In the resurrection of Osiris, Egyptians saw the pledge of a life everlasting.

For centuries the Jews believed with the Babylonians that all the dead lived in the shadowy nether world called Sheol, a world of silence, and that it was located under the Earth.

Finally, a belief in the immortality of the soul entered into Jewish thought from Hellenistic philosophy through the teachings of Plato. Plato in turn was greatly influenced by the Orphic and Eleusinian mystery religions. In *New Testament* times of Judaism, the Sadducees denied that there was any resurrection, but the Pharisees affirmed a belief in life after death long before Jesus was born.

In Islam, Muhammad conceived of the afterlife in terms of a weighing of souls, saying, "We shall place the balances of justice on the day of resurrection and no soul shall be wronged, even to the extent of a grain of mustard seed."

In Taoism and the North American Indian religions, death is approached with no fear as it is a part of the natural rhythms and cycles of the universe. And how could anything as natural as death, which follows birth, be feared?

An elderly member of the Taos pueblo used these beautiful thoughts: "Today is a very good day to die. Every living thing is in harmony with me. Every voice sings a chorus within me. All beauty has come to rest in my eyes. All bad thoughts have departed from me. Today is a very good day to die. My land is peaceful around me. My fields have been turned for the last time. My house is filled with laughter. Yes, today is a very good day to die."

The truth of death . . . and whatever truth is beyond could only be a part of the beauty of the nature and rhythm of things; of harvest and springtime; of birth, and death, and rebirth . . .

Examining Roots Of Easter

The word "Easter" does not appear in the entire Bible. The word was not Christian, and was not even used in church literature until late in the church's history. "Easter" is the name of the goddess of the spring.

Hundreds of years before Jesus was born, the spring festival was celebrated honoring "Easter," the goddess. The church borrowed the festival, and kept the goddess' name.

Even older than Easter as goddess of spring was a much wider worship and adoration of her as goddess of the dawn. In our language, the root of "Easter" is "East" — the place of dawn; and in nearly all of the languages of Northern Europe the words for Easter come from a root meaning the dawn.

Three thousand years before Jesus was born, poetic and pious Hindus kindled their morning fires, made their morning sacrifices, and sang their morning song of praise to the goddess of the dawn in ancient India. Many scholars consider the "hymn to the dawn" as among the finest of the Vedas. How they praised her, reborn in beauty in every dawn, coming with radiant face to drive away the darkness and its dangers and arouse all creatures to the joys of another day.

This was the original Easter worship, the daily praise and adoration for the dawn. It survives to this day. We still have our Easter sunrise services in every village and hamlet, a vestige of a celebration to the dawn that began 5,000 years ago, maybe longer. And 5,000 years later, we will still sing as our processional hymn on Easter Sunday in Christian churches "All creatures of our God and King, lift up your voices . . . thou burning sun with golden beam, thou rising morning . . . in praise . . . rejoice . . . alleluia."

Today we cannot even speak the word "Easter" without remembering when the Eastern sky was alive with the presence of a glorious goddess, robed in gold and purple and radiant with beauty as she rose to wake the world and call all to their morning worship.

It is worth remembering in this Easter season. It makes it far larger and more significant for me to remember how millions of people, from Iceland back to India have shared in this same worship. It places me within the larger context of the human family and brotherhood.

I like knowing that worshippers of the Christian Jesus, the Roman Jupiter, the Greek Apollo, the Norse Odin, to the Vedic Indra have all been sharing similar feelings: praise for the morning and for the spirit behind it all.

I think we can very well keep that deep feeling of praise and adoration for the miracle of the dawn. "This is the New Day which the Lord God has given us. Let us rejoice," wrote the psalmist.

In time, Easter became not just the goddess of the dawn, but the goddess of resurrection, springtime and new life.

The original celebration of the Hebrew passover celebrated by Jesus at what we know as "The Last Supper of Holy Week" was a festival of spring. And so, in the Christian church we still keep the name and keep the time every year. At the first full moon after the sun reaches the vernal equinox, the Jews still keep their ancient spring Passover. The next Sunday, Christians keep the ancient Easter. Does it not make it all far more significant and more meaningful to celebrate all of the miracles of resurrection, the mystery of life and light in this season of dawn and springtime?

God provides annually a Passover feast for every living thing on the Earth. As Jesus put it, "God makes his sun rise daily and shine on the just and the unjust alike."

God provides a feast for all of us on this Earth in swelling bud and seed. God provides a spring feast for all with a divine impartiality and allows all to feast on the glories and beauties of the resurrected earth. What a beautiful time to celebrate the resurrection of Jesus and other human spirits. Not the resurrection of a body (not even Paul went along with that), but a "spiritual" resurrection far greater than a bodily resurrection would have been.

The same truth found in that resurrected spirit can be found in countless other spirits. Albert Schweitzer was once asked the question, "Do you think that anyone has ever lived who was as good a person as Jesus?" And Schweitzer replied, "Millions."

If Christmas is symbolic of biological birth, then Easter is symbolic of spiritual birth. Easter is symbolic of the fact that the life of the spirit is timeless. There comes to me from time to time the feeling that resurrected unseen spirits, still active, still influencing, are on more solid ground than we, and that all are safe in the dimension and realities of something we can call only "eternal love."

A hundred thousand years ago somewhere on an African savannah, an eye filled with a first tear, staring past a freshly dug grave. Whence came that tear, but from the source of love, that which is eternal?

Was "love" the origin of the first dream of immortality? I think, perhaps. Love sheds its radiance upon peaceful tombs saying. "Why seek the living among the dead? They are not in tombs."

We can genuinely sing on Easter Sunday:
"All creatures of our God, lift up your voices
and with us sing . . .
thou burning sun with golden beam . . .
thou rising morning . . . in praise, rejoice.
Alleluia!"

There Can Be No Easter
Without Love In Our Hearts

Thousands and thousands of years before the *Bible* was written, or Jesus was born, love filled human hearts and dreamed of immortality.

A number of years ago, while enjoying a vacation tucked away in a little cabin on the Olympic Peninsula of Washington, I was informed of the death of one of Tacoma's most beloved people. I arose about three a.m. the next morning to prepare my spirit for the funeral meditation that I soon would be presenting.

I walked out of my cabin, nestled in fir and hemlock, and stepped onto the Pacific beach into a mystical dimension that is beyond my language or vocabulary to describe. The highest modes of experience always transcend the reach of any language.

The moon was full, hanging fragile, like a Japanese lantern. The reflection on the softly breaking surf, dissolving into lace like mist, touched my soul and spirit more than all the words humankind has written in sacred literature.

And thoughts began to lay gently on my mind; there came a vision of a death, somewhere in the distant, distant past, thousands and thousands of years ago, on perhaps an African savannah at the dawn of humanity. Staring into space past that grave, filled with flowers, a first tear filled eyes.

Whence came that first tear flowing out of a heart having experienced love? Whence came the first sob in the throat but from the source of love, that which is eternal? And today still, the mystery of life and death, two mysteries which are yet one remain.

Life and death are equal kings. Presidents and babes lie side by side. Kings and peasants share the same soil. Every birth asks: Whence came thou? Every grave asks: Whither goest thou? The most unlettered person weeping over his loved one can answer the questions of this mystery equally as well as the most learned scholar in his study, for we are all equal, as we stand, with tears in our eyes, before a loved one's grave.

The mystery of love remains. Humans have intuitively sensed, from religious mystic to philosopher, poet and musician, that it is through something we call "love" that this mystery we call "God" is most deeply experienced on this planet we call "Earth."

And there is more; in this love there is no fear, whether in this life or that new reality beyond this life. No person, standing before this mystery has the wisdom or the knowledge to see across the curtain. But for those who stand before their dead with aching hearts, one affirmation endures, one truth remains and one light shines clear. Where there has been love, there has been life. Where there has been love, there has been God. And it has been almost a universal experience of human kind, expressed in multiple ways by many religions that: Where love is, God is.

This love was not born of the *Bible.* Its birthplace was the human heart where, for thousands upon thousands of years with all peoples in all cultures, it has brought joy; built hope; been the mother of beauty; overcome fear and given a richness and significance to the living of days that would otherwise have been absent.

It has been almost universal in religious mythologies that love brought order out of chaos, light out of darkness. Love is the perfume and the fragrance of the soul. "In love there is no fear, therefore let not your heart be troubled and neither let it be afraid."

Prior to his death, the author and poet, Archibald MacLeish said that his Pulitzer Prize-winning play *J. B.* was the finest thing he had ever written. He re-wrote the ending four times before he knew he had the final answer. (J. B. is a modern businessman who plays out the suffering of the biblical Job.)

J. B.'s wife, Sarah, says to him, "Let us blow on the coals of our hearts and we'll see by and by, we'll see where we are and we'll know." And J. B., with great difficulty answers: "God answered me like the stillness of a star that silences us asking, Sarah. We are. We just are and that is our answer. And what we are can suffer, and what suffers loves. And love will live its suffering again; risk its own defeat again, endure loss again, and yet again and again . . . and yet, still live and still love."

"To love God and neighbor as oneself is much more than all offerings and all sacrifices; and is the greatest commandment of all" said one scribe to Jesus. And to the same scribe, Jesus replied, "You are not far from the kingdom of God."

There can be no Easter in our lives until there is Easter in our hearts . . . love, resurrected.

THE BRIDGE

We love this bridge on the Lake Fork Creek. We thought it the perfect symbol for the final section of this book as we head into an uncharted and unknown future.

There is a path leading to the bridge, but on the other side there is none, only grass and woods. If you care to walk further, you must find your own way and make your own path toward your own destination. So it is in our individual religious quest; we must go alone, listening to our own heart. "Them as hunts treasure must go alone, and at night, and leave a little of their own blood behind them" said a girl of the Pacific Islands to Loren Eiseley. And so it is as we seek the greatest treasure of all . . . "that Kingdom where not even a sparrow falls to the ground unknown and where the least shall be considered side by side with the greatest". . . It takes courage and involves risk, the breaking of a fresh trail after crossing the bridge . . . but such has always been the case with those who have pointed their lives . . . toward the Mystery.

TOWARD THE FUTURE

"A man never rises so high as when he know not whither he is going."
— *Oliver Cromwell*

"Nothing is secure but life . . . transition . . . the energizing spirit. No love can be bound by oath or covenant to secure it against a higher love. No truth so sublime but it may be trivial tomorrow in the light of new thoughts. People wish to be settled . . . only so far as they are unsettled is there any hope."
— *Emerson*

"How many ideas there have been on earth in the history of man which were unthinkable ten years before they appeared. YET WHEN THEIR DESTINED HOUR HAD COME, THEY CAME FORTH AND SPREAD OVER THE WHOLE EARTH."
— *Dostoevsky: Brothers Karamazov*

"Beauty is the inseparable characteristic of the idea when it has become known. In other words, everything is beautiful in which an idea is revealed, for to be beautiful means no more than clearly to express an idea . . . whose time has come."
— *Schopenhauer*

"Great thinkers use common words to say very uncommon things. Small thinkers try to wrap up trivial ideas in grand words . . . and to clothe their very common and ordinary thought in the most far-fetched expressions. If a man wants to get great ideas he must read great books and great thinkers, and avoid like the plague the others; for life is short and time and energy limited."
— *Schopenhauer: Style*

Gift Of Laughter Can Refresh Faith

At one of the most serious times of the war, Abraham Lincoln turned to the members of his cabinet and said, "Laugh, gentlemen . . . Laugh, or you will go mad."

Abraham Lincoln's favorite stories were what he called his "preacher jokes." Needless to say, the clergy of that day did not find many of them very funny.

Too many in the church forget that laughter is a sacred gift that can refresh the soul. I remember one of the most delightful scenes in the Old Testament when Abraham and Sarah, both of them, laugh at God. God wants to know, "What's so funny?"

Abraham and Sarah thought it was hilarious what God wanted of them at their age. Abraham was 100 years old and Sarah was 90 years old, and here God wanted them to have a child. This certainly would be the height of optimism and humor.

Abraham fell down on his face, rolling with laughter at God, and said "Do you mean that we can have a child at our age? Do you know how old we are?" They laughed, even at God.

The Hebrew writers thought that God often laughed. Would we not all be better off and far healthier spiritually and emotionally if we would, even as Abraham, laugh at God more often? And laugh at our religious pretensions?

Why were, and are, so many of our Church "fathers" opposed to laughing at much of the church and the clergy? Do they sense that laughter might weaken the somber, grim fabric of their creeds?

Or maybe they know, many of them, deep within their hearts that they are in some sense laughable. Laughter can strip away excessive dignity and presumptuous titles.

I, for instance, am always joking about the pretense and presumptuousness of ministerial titles such as "The Right Reverend" or "The Very Most Right Reverend" or "The Very Most Often Right Reverend Doctor." I do this often around my ministerial colleagues. Not many see any humor in it, sadly.

Laughter has the redeeming quality of being able to strip away pretensions, suffocating seriousness and excessive dignity.

When our puffed up pride and fragile egos and sterile self-importance are deflated, then a sweet humility might enter our lives.

When we can honestly look at ourselves and laugh, we become more of the "real stuff," as Carl Jung used to say.

Laughter can restore reality. Laughter is a natural sacrament of life. To be able to laugh at one another can redeem families.

Whatever, or whomever, made "man" and the universe made laughter, too. Laughter can be a challenge to the unknown.

The Hebrew writers who gave us the Old Testament section of the Bible thought it perfectly natural to laugh at God, and thought it natural for God to laugh back.

And Abraham fell on his face, rolling with laughter at God, saying "Do you mean that a 100-year-old man and a 90-year-old woman can have a baby? Even Sarah is laughing."

And God said, "Why not?"

And God, Abraham and Sarah, all three, must have laughed together at each other . . . and with each other.

"A human being should live only in harmony with his very own nature . . . and according to his own nature. He should live in accordance with the truth about himself."
– Carl Jung

"The seeker of his truest . . . deepest self must pick out the ONE on which to stake his salvation."
– Wm. James

"A truly creative person has little power over his own life. He is captive and driven by his creative energies."
– Carl Jung

"Naturally . . . nature has so disposed me."
– Leonardo da Vinci

"I determined from that moment on . . . never again to let anyone push me . . . in any direction . . . not in harmony with my own nature."
– Carl Jung

"All my clients ask . . . basically . . . the same thing . . . 'How can I live in harmony with my real self . . . underneath all of my surface behavior?'"
– Erich Fromm

"There must come a time in one's life . . . when he finally says . . . 'This is me . . . and the rest of the world can go to hell.'"
– Dostoevsky

Appreciate The Grace
Of The Present Moment

Martha was the busiest woman in Bethany. Can you not identify with her, lady of today? She scrubbed, swept and dusted; washed, ironed, baked and roasted; basted and tasted; she belonged to PTA, five church organizations and four civic organizations; she did her time with the Boy Scouts, Girl Scouts and the 4-H; she had the butcher and the baker on her weekly list; and she kept everything well-organized.

On one particular evening, Jesus was with Martha's sister, Mary, visiting in the cool of the day on the front porch. (The shank of the evening, as my grandmother used to say.) From within the house came an increasing clatter of plates and pots, pans and jugs, knives and forks . . . and, finally, Martha, hands dripping, face red, appeared angrily on the door sill saying, "It must be wonderful just sitting out there on the porch visiting."

"Oh Martha, you are so anxious and so troubled about so many things," said Jesus, "but only one thing is needful."

To Martha, it was 7 p.m. in the evening, her time, and a schedule was to be kept. Mary thought differently. The time was God's eternal time, and this person might never come again. Pots and pans would wait. (My secretary wants to know why they did not help with the dishes. But that's another column.)

I have often thought, what a blessing that Jesus did not have an appointment book or a wrist watch. He would have missed 90 percent of the people along the way that he came to know so well.

The woman at the well of Samaria might never have heard of the springs of living water. I can hear it now as Jesus looked at his wrist watch, "Sorry lady, but I have to be at the temple in 10 minutes for a meeting of the Chamber of Commerce and following that is a meeting of the Greater Downtown Ministerial Alliance, and tonight I have two board meetings. Maybe I can work you in next week for 10 minutes or so. Let me get my little calendar out of my briefcase here and see what meetings I have next week."

We live in a world where the clock, the wrist watch and the appointment calendar rule our days and our lives. It is relatively recent in origin. Time has become linear, and progress is measured by a calendar and a full appointment book directing us in a straight line, linear, toward a goal or objective.

Respect for the clock and appointment book often reaches idolatry. If you dare to be silent and still for a moment, as you sit there behind your desk, pause and ask: "Why am I doing this? What is it all for? Did I come into this world with a soul, which may very likely be immortal, for the sole purpose of sitting behind this desk every day, eight hours a day, five days a week, for 40 years, following the clock and the appointment book?"

If you reflect for very long on those questions, I guarantee you that a void will open up under your padded chair. But more importantly, you might have a chance to rediscover the moment; the eternal now.

Human beings who are oriented and preoccupied almost continually with the past and the future seldom experience the human and spiritual possibilities inherent in the fullness of one's being and living in the now. Is there not something frantic about the way many of us live? We are like a person in bed with a fever, constantly changing our positions to relieve the pain. Does not your mind reel with the activities that have mastered you? "Quiet desperation" Thoreau called it.

I am writing of the grace of the present moment which can cut into our linear and chronological time and give us a new perspective. George Santayana was lecturing one morning to his philosophy class at Harvard University. After about 10 minutes, he stopped, and looking through the open windows, said to his class, "Gentlemen, it is springtime. The Earth is alive. The forsythia is in bloom and that is far, far more important than philosophy. Let us go walking."

The significance of our activities is to be found only in an awareness of the depth of eternity, in which we are having our few brief seconds on this planet. We seldom think such thoughts. We just work on, following the clock, the appointment book, considering the past and thinking of the future. Five o'clock finally comes and work is done. Another day is gone, and we begin to arm ourselves against the empty hours . . . by planning our appointments for . . . tomorrow.

Why Do We Wait To Express Love?

In the past few years I have been touched by the death of my father. One thought kept coming back into my mind, one question, and that is the question I am asking you now.

Why do we wait, the majority of us, until the last week of someone's life to tell them what they have meant to us?

"What grieves me now in this time of pain," wrote the poet Clark Moustakas to his wife, "is that I never before put my feelings, my sacred valuing of you, into words."

Why did I wait until the last week to lean down over my 90-pound father, who was racked with cancer, to whisper to him "Dad, you have been a great father, thank you so much, I love you very much."

The tears that filled his eyes, as barely, lightly, from shriveled lips, he forced a response with words that I could not remember having heard, "I love you too, son." Why do we wait?

We have been told by the authors of The Book that God is love, and wherever love is, God is. Now if that be true, and I believe it is, then where love enters a life, God has entered that life, whether Christian, Jew, Hindu, Buddhist, Taoist, whatever. For wherever love is, God is.

In the *Book of John*, the author even makes it stronger. "If you say you know God, but do not love, you are a liar." Even Jesus needed to be loved, lest we forget. One of the most poignant lines he ever uttered, apparently in a time of abject loneliness was: "Foxes have holes, birds have nests, but the Son of Man has nowhere to lay his head." He was rejected by his parents and his hometown, who thought him "beside himself."

One of the most tender and touching scenes from *Jesus Christ, Superstar* is the comfort that Mary Magdalene gives to Jesus, singing the haunting *I Don't Know How to Love Him*. Any number of fine Biblical scholars have said that the interpretation could be historically close to the truth, for Mary was the last one with him before his death, and the first to whom he appeared following his death.

We all need to give love and to receive love. A general and hazy "brotherly" love of "mankind" is an abstraction. Love in such a generalized sense can only be a very thin and diluted thought. It is not normal or natural for me to "love" a few million persons across an ocean. Why is it that "love" always increases in direct proportion to the distance involved? We step and stumble all over the bodies of those around us daily, while looking across an ocean for someone to "love."

You and I may be able to "feel" for the human beings across the ocean in a very abstract and very distant way. But that feeling cannot change lives, redeem lives, heal lives, save lives and give a new joy and new significance to lives. You can do it by putting that feeling into words and actions for those who need to be told — now.

"If I had known what trouble you were bearing, I would have lent a little love to you, and slipped my hand within your hand, and made your stay more pleasant in the land — if I had known."

– Clark Moustakas

"Life is streaming into our cells . . . from the universe outside . . . and the light from all of our cells is streaming out . . . throughout the entire universe. Each of us is broadcasting a symphony to each other. My atomic and energy waves . . . are mingling with yours right now . . . yours with mine . . . all tied mysteriously to the core of our earth. I am filled at this moment with the waves from the farthest nebula. Distance is total illusion. So is time. The essence of the farthest star is here in me . . . just as our essence is a part of the farthest star . . . and throughout the entire universe.

Every thought that you have is being stamped on the record of the universe. We are writing our lives on the pages of eternity . . . as space is illusion . . . so is time. Time is illusion. Somehow . . . we are projecting ourselves into the eternal . . . stepping through the door into a dimension that is all truth and all love.

We must change the patterns of our thinking . . . in order to reach the truth . . . of our existence . . . the truth of reality. We are entering an age . . . of a new reality."

– from the writing of Dr. Donald
Andrews, Professor Emeritus of
Chemistry, Johns Hopkins
University; Distinguished Professor
of Chemistry, University of Florida;
Consultant to Los Alamos
Laboratory for Atomic Energy

How Do We Heed Message Of Love

For how many have religious laws and rules, vested interests and institutions, replaced the needs of people? Nothing in his time, it seems, so infuriated Jesus.

It was against the law to feed or to heal a human being on the Sabbath. Traditional laws were more important than people. Quite bluntly Jesus let them know that "The Sabbath was made for people . . . people were not made for the Sabbath," (*Mark 2:27*).

This is the final test for all institutions, including the church and religious institutions. The validity of every institution lies outside of itself. Does it feed, fill, enrich, restore and redeem people? If it does not, it has failed. People are sacred. Institutions are not sacred, nor are religious laws, doctrines or theology.

Have you noticed how little many care for people, as long as they get their point across? Even if people suffer, as long as they won the debate, they are happy and satisifed.

I have often wondered what it would be like, if someday, somewhere, we meet our Great Spirit face to face and we open the meeting by telling "Him" of all the large programs we exhausted ourselves with . . . and all of the gigantic plans we labored for . . . and all of the grand public projects we gave ourselves to, only to hear the question asked of us, "But . . . the bodies, the bodies, the bodies of all those around you that were crushed, where are they? All of the lonely who cried for a word of love, a touch and an arm around their shoulder, where are they?"

I would like for you to think of something this week. For close to 2,000 years of our Christian institution, the church, thousands upon thousands of people have been tortured, butchered and executed for not believing in the prevailing doctrines and creeds of the time.

But in all of those years, to my knowledge, not one, not ONE person has ever been tried by an ecclesiastical court and put to death for not obeying the Great Commandment, "To love neighbor as self." Not one person has ever been sentenced for not loving enough.

He comes to us as he came to those of old, by the lakeside, and he says to us the same words . . . "Follow thou me," and we ask, "Where?" "Why," he says, "To all of those people you are stumbling over daily, to the Marys and the Marthas and the woman of the well, to the prostitute and the tax collector, to the Mary Magdalenes and the fisherman by the lakeside, to those sharing in the wine and the joy of the wedding party, to the Pilates and the Peters and to Nicodemus, and through the people you will find who it is that you follow."

Who and what is in need of people? Only other people. It is people who need people. Do the mountains stand in need of our poems?

Would the stars fade away if astronomers ceased to exist? Would the birds stop singing if musicians and artists stopped writing music and painting? Nature does not need us. Nature cannot satisfy our most basic need, the need of being needed. "We are children needing other children, and yet letting our grown up pride hide all the need inside, acting more like children than children" (from the song, *People*).

There is not one in this world who loves the outdoors more than I. I thrill to the woods, to nature, and have known the joys of ocean and mountains in backpacking and hiking. And yet . . . nature is not the final and ultimate joy that makes one's heart sing.

No mountain has yet said to me, "Don't cry, it will be all right."

No sunset touches and takes my hand and says, "I love you."

No tree has yet said, "May I help you with your problem?"

No flower has said, "Neither do I condemn thee."

No moon nor star can put an arm around my shoulder and say, "We will go through this thing together . . . you and I."

And a scribe said to Jesus, "To love God and neighbor is more than all the sacrifices and offerings." And Jesus said to that scribe, "You are not far from the Kingdom of God." The scribe had only mentioned one thing, love . . . love for God and people.

A church should say only one thing: "Follow truth as you find it, but come with me to the man of Nazareth and let us look at the Great Commandment of Judaism, underlined by him, to love God and neighbor, and see what it is trying to say.

"What do we know? Only this: that we have the same needs, and we are brothers and sisters. Come then, let us bow our heads before the Eternal Thou, before the Divine Rhythm, the Divine Flow of the universe that we call . . . God. And then let us rise up and help one another as we pass upon our way."

"Voluntary Euthanasia" Can Be An Ethical Way Out

One of the most respected men in the Christian church, as scholar, teacher and administrator, was Dr. Henry Pitney Van Dusen, president of the prestigious Union Theological Seminary in New York City. He enjoyed a reputation that was worldwide.

Dr. Van Dusen suffered a stroke, and lost his voice completely. His wife was in severe arthritic condition. They had long supported the concept of voluntary euthanasia. ("Suicide" if you want to call it that; I like voluntary euthanasia.) And so, in January 1975 they made their decision. Together, they took a large dose of sleeping pills and went to bed. They left behind a note for all of us. It read:

"Nowadays it is difficult to die. We feel that this way we are taking will become more usual and acceptable as the years pass."

Many persons who have never thought this subject through and who have thoughtlessly accepted the old wives' tales and cliches about suicide, were stunned. But Norman Cousins, the editor of the *Saturday Review*, wrote one of his most penetrating editorials, and made an observation that is devastating in its clarity, logic and wisdom. He asked this question: "Why are people more appalled by what they term an unnatural form of dying, than by an unnatural form of living?"

The German philosopher, Schopenhauer, said it very well: "The clergy should once and for all be challenged to give an account, with what right they stigmatize in the pulpit . . . and in their writings an action committed voluntarily by many . . . there is no Biblical authority that gives them such rights." And he was right.

There are four suicides in the Old Testament, and there is not one word of adverse comment made about any of them. In the New Testament, the suicide of even Judas is merely recorded without comment, and is not listed as one of his so-called "crimes."

It is time we moved on past the archaic views of voluntary euthanasia and see it for what it can be, as Dr. and Mrs. Van Dusen so indicated. It is not an act of "cowardice," as the old cliche goes. It can, and often is, a most courageous act made from a sound mind and a mind of wisdom, as in the case of the Van Dusens.

There are more and more people of great intelligence and wisdom today saying voluntary euthanasia made from a sound mind is a valid moral and ethical option for each of us. Do these words cause you to cringe?

Then consider the alternative. There are hundreds of thousands of persons today in the United States living in continuing sustained misery, pain, and anguish. Thousands literally imprisoned in nursing homes and hospitals; other thousands isolated, left alone, family gone, just prolonging lonely, miserable days.

How many of us have said, "It won't happen to me. It won't happen to me." How many hundreds, literally hundreds, of times, have people said to me . . . after having viewed such a sick miserable person chained to a bed by tubes, "Not that way for me. I want to die on the tennis court, the ski slopes, the golf course, active . . . with all my facilities working." Then, if they do die quickly, painlessly, active, how many of us say, "My, what a blessing — he—she didn't have to suffer." Well, the obvious question is, "Why should anyone have to suffer?"

I might not die on the ski slope, or the tennis or squash court active and alert. I might end up senile, feeble, sick, imprisoned in a bed in pain and misery, alone except for an attendant doctor and an attendant nurse. Before that time arrives, I would hope that I would have the option for my own voluntary euthanasia . . . with dignity and peace of mind, freely with no excuses, no regrets, and no explanation needed.

I know one thing. I would be in very good company. The list of outstanding men and women of wisdom who chose voluntary euthanasia could run into dozens of pages. If you want to begin with Socrates and move on through Seneca and Paula, Demosthenes, Lucretius, Hannibal, Brutus, Cassius, Mark Anthony and Cleopatra, and through kings and queens of royalty in Persia and Cyprus to Ernest Hemingway and Dr. and Mrs. Henry Pitney Van Dusen.

Is it not true that we are talking about the ultimate freedom and the final liberty . . . to remain in control of one's own life and one's own death . . . and who has the wisdom to deprive us of that? I ask you a question: "Is physical survival under any condition, no matter how appalling, to be valued over individual liberty? Is choosing death not a live, valid option where freedom exists?"

In your quiet moments, pause, reflect upon it and meditate upon it; much of our orthodox thinking on the subject becomes questionable.

The great Dane, Soren Kierkegaard, theologian and philosopher, asks this question, "What is reflection? Only this, simply to reflect on these two questions:

"How did I get into this world . . .

And how do I get out of it again . . .

How does it all end for me?

"What is thoughtlessness," he asked, "to muster everything in order to drown all thought about entrance . . .

And my exit."

"Uncommon" People, Please Step Forward

I have never understood the worship and adulation of the "common man" in our culture. The word "common" in *Webster's Dictionary* means: "crude, without distinction, second rate, inferior, cheap, trite, below normal, unrefined and inelegant."

What greater insult than to be known as a common person. We praise commonness, and yet not one of us wants to be treated by a common doctor or have our life defended by a common lawyer. We want excellence.

Before he died, Ernest Hemingway called this "the millenium of the untalented." He said: "We are surrounded by actors who cannot act . . . singers who cannot sing . . . writers who cannot write . . . teachers who cannot teach . . . speakers who cannot speak, and painters who cannot paint." And we pay them fortunes for their mediocrity.

One of the early Greek poets put it this way: "Before the gates of excellence the high gods have placed sweat." Contemporary author and scholar Eric Hoffer used these words: "Those who lack talent expect things to happen without effort. They ascribe failure to a lack of inspiration or ability, or to misfortune rather than to insufficient application. Thus, talent is a species of vigor."

Why do we so fear demanding excellence in the schools or one's life and vocation? Several years ago, the 82-year-old Seattle maestro, Dr. Stanley Chapple, was invited to direct a performance of the Tacoma Youth Symphony. And what an education it was for those high school young people — an education far more important than the music they were playing.

Dr. Chapple stood in front of the orchestra at the first rehearsal and said: "I will demand that you rise to my standards of music excellence. I will most certainly not bend down to your level. I will treat you as if you were the Boston Symphony or the New York Philharmonic. I will direct as if you were professional musicians. I demand that you rise to excellence. Now, let us begin."

On performance night, the quality and majesty of the production exceeded all expectations.

"People do not stumble into excellence," wrote John Gardner, "but all excellence involves application and tenacity of purpose. An excellent plumber is infinitely more admirable than an incompetent lawyer or doctor" (teacher or minister, I would add).

How often do we hide our commonness in the sanctuary of groups. We say, "I'm with them, even if they are wrong, I am with the AMA or the ADA, the rural group or the city group, the Republicans or Democrats, the Presbyterians or Episcopalians, the NAACP or the American Legion. I'll vote with them, even if what they are doing is idiotic." This is called "salvation by survey." The common person surveys his group and the polls to get his beliefs and his cue.

And too, we commonize our existence with meaningless cliches such as "moderation in all things." Moderation is the key to mediocrity. Moderation is defined as "staying within accepted limits." Uncommon people who are memorable and who use their time on this Earth to the fullest are usually most immoderate and never stay within the accepted limits.

The Sadducees and the Pharisees stayed within the accepted limits of Hebrew law. Jesus did neither. He immoderately loved those whom the Pharisees despised, and he immoderately shattered a great many of their rules and traditions. The creative giants of civilization, in all disciplines, have forgotten themselves into immortality by vast immoderate creativity and contributions and by never staying within accepted limits.

The uncommon person is never embarrassed in letting others know that excellence has one of the highest priorities in life. "You do not hide your light under a basket," said Jesus, "but you place it on top of a hill where all can see." For the person seeking excellence to hide their light, or pretend it is not there, is absurd, ridiculous and wrong. The uncommon person resents the continued acceptance of laziness, mediocrity and ignorance and resents any educational or social system that promotes such.

Our communities, our school systems, our churches, our very culture is crying for such excellence and perhaps dying for lack of it.

The Reagan administration is asking that $1.6 trillion be spent in fiscal years 1983-1987 on our military budget. Could it be that far more important to our national salvation would be a new and serious commitment to a higher standard of individual and collective excellence as exemplified by our founding fathers? A rededication to a quality of life?

If we, as a people, have no dreams, goals, ideas or thoughts that have to do with human excellence and human distinction, then we are the most to be pitied and the most pathetic. It is time for all potentially excellent men and women to come to the aid of their party . . . whose name is Western civilization.

"Normal" Times Always Seem Uncertain

Writing at the end of Old Testament history, when the Hebrews were experiencing political upheaval, reversal of fortunes, spiritual depression and hopelessness, the author of *Ecclesiastes* wrote these words: "The thing that hath been, it is that which shall be; and that which is done, is that which shall be done."

The author is saying that the conditions of life are not that unusual or new.

The majority of us, I am sure, have the impression that we are living in abnormal times. We see crisis piled on top of crisis, from inflation to strained international relations. But the historian and the anthropologist would say that we are living in perfectly "normal" times.

My life, as an example, has been perfectly "normal," as has yours. I was born close to the end of World War I. I endured with my parents the Depression, saw the dust bowl days of Oklahoma, and lived with the exploits of "Pretty Boy" Floyd, John Dillinger and Bonnie and Clyde. My children were born during World War II, when Hitler was marching. I was a father during the days of the Berlin airlift, the Korean conflict, the cold war and Vietnam. I helped my country in two conflicts as a U.S. Marine Corps pilot in World War II and Korea. And I philosophized with my son as his time came for military duty.

Do you see what I am saying? All of my life I have been waiting for normal times, when all of my life I have been living in normal times.

It's like the doctor asking the patient, "Have you had this illness before?"

"Yes," said the patient.

"Well, said the doctor, "you've got it again." And so it is.

Recognizing that these are perfectly normal times, I ask, "What can I depend on in these uncertain, normal times? Is there any solid ground anywhere beneath my feet?"

In a seeming paradox I find my answer in Emerson: "Nothing is secure but life, change and the energizing spirit. No love can be bound by oath or covenant to secure it against a higher love. No truth so sublime, but that it may be trivial tomorrow in the light of new thoughts." In harmony with these thoughts is Cromwell's observation, "No one rises so high as he who knows NOT where he is going."

Well, you say, good grief, Edelen, how could that give you any comfort? I think of many of the great individuals in history who rose to magnificent heights, remaining true and committed to their vision, not knowing where they were going. I am sure that Buddha, Moses, Socrates, or even Jesus never really could see the outcome of their vision.

Do we really think that the Greeks in the age of Pericles knew

135

where they were going, or Europe in the Renaissance, or the Founding Fathers of this great nation of ours?

Our Founding Fathers could not have known. They knew only the general direction and *on that* they staked "their lives and their fortunes and their sacred honor." They transformed their own days into enriching dimensions and rose to splendid heights knowing that "nothing is secure," and "not knowing where they were going."

Sensing that it could not all be achieved in one lifetime, they were saved by hope; and sensing that the good and the beautiful could not make complete sense in that immediate context, they were saved by faith; and sensing that nothing we do can be accomplished alone, they were saved by love. The destination can never be known, only the general direction. Living our days in faith hope and love, we can rise to new heights and pledge our lives, our fortunes and our sacred honor to our own vision in our own normal, perilous times.

Not too many years ago, deep in a cave in Spain, a young girl was walking ahead of her father, a paleontologist. Suddenly she yelled with delight, "Toro, Toro." And there, on the ceiling of that cave, were paintings of bison that were exquisite in design and form. There was nothing crude about them. These paintings were done 20,000 years ago in what must have seemed like terribly abnormal, perilous times.

It would seem that survival would have been all that mattered, with great ice flows, predators, starvation, cold and disease. And yet, there in that cave, squatting on his haunches, a lover of the beautiful, a sensitive artist, rose from that rubbled floor, squinted through a sputtering torch, and painted works of beauty that have endured for 20,000 normal, perilous years.

May we, in our own normal, perilous times, living by the same hope, the same faith, create some beauty . . . in our own place.

How Proud I Am To Be Known As A Liberal

I have often heard myself referred to as "liberal." I cannot tell you how proud I am to be known by that classification. It is one of the most beautiful and cherished words in our language. It has nothing to do, really, with whether you are a Republican or Democrat, a Unitarian, Presbyterian or Congregationalist. It has to do with an attitude, a frame of mind, an orientation to life and events, a philosophy, a concept, having to do with freedom. Liberal and liberty both have the same root, defined in *Webster's Dictionary* as: "The quality or state of being free . . . as a freeman . . . a free person; as opposed to slavery, bondage and subjection; worthy of a man of free birth; not servile or mean; a noble way, generous, open-handed; free from bigotry . . . inclined to welcome new ideas." If liberalism is that which liberates, which sets free the minds, spirits and bodies of human beings, then how proud I am to be known as one who is dedicated to such a noble concept.

The object of liberalism is to free those caught in the chains of political, social and religious bondage. At the heart of a liberal religion is something called faith. A person demonstrates faith not by believing anything, but by living. In a liberal religion, a person arrives at his position through his own reason and experiences and not because of some outside authority. Faith is the centering point for both the liberal person and the liberal church. We live our faith in our freedom. We move through our faith to freedom, "Keeping abreast of truth," as our great hymn, *Once To Every Man and Nation* puts it.

This attitude threatens those who want to deify the past and live there and keep trying like ventriloquists to speak for a 2,000-year-old age in which they never lived. They reject all contemporary and biblical scholarship and any discovery that cuts the ground out from under their traditional religious and biblical beliefs, while like schizophrenics, they want all the benefits of contemporary knowledge and science in those areas that save their lives and heal their bodies.

They do not reject the joys of telephones, television, jet plane travel or antibiotics. Those wanting ancient and archaic religious beliefs are more than eager to accept the contemporary scholarship that saves their lives in hospital beds, while at the same time denouncing all research that throws too blinding a light on their Bible and religious beliefs. If it seems that God is calling them to heaven, but antibiotics would keep them around a little longer on Earth, they show an eager preference for the pagan and heathen benefits of antibiotics.

They do not want to die under a medieval, archaic King James doctor. But they would ask us to live by medieval King James religious beliefs. If science and scholarship provides them with healing vaccines, they say that is God's will working through the research scientists and doctors. But when that same wicked science and scholarship indicates that their Bible and religious beliefs will not hold water, nor their creeds, then all of a sudden, that same science and scholarship becomes the work of the devil, humanists and liberals. It's like when it comes to religion and their Bible, they all of a sudden have had a frontal lobotomy.

Truth is more holy than any creed; more sacred than any dogma. The true religious liberal respects only that theology that can hold up in the forum of unsheltered truth and that can be justified in the light of all contemporary academic and scholastic research regardless of where it leads, and regardless of what cherished convictions must be relinquished. Any system other than this is to keep human minds and spirits in chains and fetters; in other words . . . bondage.

It is worth being redundant to define liberalism again: "To set free from bondage and subjection; that which liberates . . . devotion to freedom."

There is a religion that says freedom: freedom from ignorance and superstition; freedom to seek truth wherever it leads; freedom to follow honest thought; freedom to seek the holy dimensions of human existence with minds and spirits unimpaired by paralyzing authoritarianism and indoctrination. To be liberal is to move through faith to freedom.

I am very proud to represent freedom and the future and to be known as liberal. "He who looks back is not fit for the kingdom. God is God of the living, not the dead," Jesus said. The face of the one and only living God is ever set toward tomorrow for "time makes ancient good uncouth, and they must upward and onward who would keep abreast of truth."

The Future Requires Courage

We live in an exciting and stimulating period of history. One age is dying . . . and the new age is not quite born.

We see radical changes in sexual patterns, lifestyles, marriage styles, women's roles, family structures, education, energy, religion, the Christian church and in almost every conceivable aspect of life. We can withdraw in anxiety, or we can become negative and pessimistic. If we choose either of these paths, we forfeit our chance to participate in the creation of the future.

To live in this age, or any age, requires an enormous amount of courage, faith and willingness to take risks. But to participate in the forming of a future is to create. And courage, risk-taking, creativity and faith are the attributes that have continually reformed the structure of civilization.

What is creative courage? It is the willingness to pursue new forms, new symbols and new patterns of truth. The alternative is stagnation.

Every profession — technology, diplomacy, business, arts, medicine, law — requires those who possess a creative courage. Certainly that is true in teaching and the ministry.

At the end of *A Portrait of the Artist as a Young Man,* James Joyce has his young hero write these words in his diary: "Welcome O Life . . . I go to encounter for the millionth time the reality of experience and to forge in the smithy of my soul the uncreated conscience of my race."

In other words, every creative encounter is a new event, and every time requires another assertion of courage and faith and involves risk. I especially like the words, "to forge . . . the uncreated conscience of my race." Joyce is saying here that conscience is not something handed down ready-made from Mount Sinai, nor the Sermon on the Mount, given once and for all.

Why is creativity so difficult? Why does it require such courage? Why is it such a risk-taking venture? For the very reason that it does contribute to the process of creating a new conscience for the race. It is not just simply a matter of clearing out debris from an ancient age, of clearing away dead norms, defunct symbols and myths that have become lifeless. It is not that simple.

The major risk is that creativity provokes the jealousy of the institutional gods. That is why genuine, authentic creativity always takes such courage.

An active battle with the gods occurs, whether the gods be an institution, a church, a government, or those protecting an outmoded image of a supernatural God. Courageous creativity always provokes the jealousy of, and outrages, the gods. In ancient Greek civilization Prometheus challenged Zeus, and Zeus was outraged. The same truth was presented in the myth of Adam and Eve. "God" is outraged at the audacious courage of Adam and Eve.

The relating of rebellion and creative courage to religion is hard for many people to swallow. In religion it has not been, by and large, the flatterers of the popular God who have been ultimately praised. It has been the insurgents and the rebels who are praised by history and immortalized, among them Socrates, Jesus and Joan of Arc.

The pharaoh of the 18th dynasty of Egypt, Akhnaton, challenged the entire corrupt priesthood of Egypt saying, "You are enslaving people with your superstitions . . . your ignorant beliefs." Zoroaster was persecuted; Buddha made scathing attacks upon Hindu corruption in his time; Luther and Schweitzer were excommunicated from their church.

The biblical prophet Micah had the courage to speak: "There is no anthropomorphic god up there waiting for your sacrifices and rites and rituals. No. All that is required of you is to do justly and love mercy and to walk humbly."

In one of Renan's philosphical dramas there is a dialogue in heaven where Gabriel speaking of the Earth and its skeptics says to God . . . "if I had thine omnipotence, I would quickly reduce those wicked atheists to silence." But God, benevolently replies: "Ah Gabriel, thou art so faithful, but thy faithfulness has made thee so narrow. Learn my special tenderness for those who deny me. For what they deny is the image, grotesque and abominable which has been put in my place. In all the world of idolaters, they alone, the doubters and deniers, are the only ones who really respect me."

The cemeteries of history are filled with the graves of the dead gods . . . Astarte, Baal, Isis, Horus, Osiris, Jupiter, Thor. It is time to bury at least one other god, the god of vengeance and anger, a theological policeman whose beat is the universe, a heavenly trigger man, a celestial hit man who has a contract out on some earthly humans.

There is a far greater archaeology than digging for lost cities. It is an archaeology of the mind, aimed at uncovering the foundations of the authentic city of the soul, covered with all the debris of conventional and antiquated religious systems. We must dig through, layer by layer, until once again each of us can experience in our own lives the fresh new spirit that speaks again "let there be light . . . and there was light . . ."

ABOUT THE AUTHOR

William Edelen was born in West Texas and spent his boyhood there and in Oklahoma City. He flew for twelve years as a U.S. Marine Corps pilot, flying both fighter planes and transports in World War II and Korea. He requested a discharge and returned to Oklahoma State University where he received the Bachelor of Science degree in Horticulture. He then entered McCormick Theological Seminary (on the campus of the University of Chicago) where he received his Master of Theology degree. After serving Presbyterian churches for six years he received a grant to do further studies in the Graduate School of Anthropology, the University of Colorado. Concluding two years there he returned to the active ministry in the United Church of Christ (Congregational). He taught for seven years at the University of Puget Sound in Tacoma, Washington, Comparative Religion and Anthropology. During those same years he was the minister of the First Congregational Church in Tacoma. Since 1981 he has been the minister of the Community Congregational Church in McCall, Idaho. He and his wife founded THE SYMPOSIUM of McCall, an organization to promote the humanities and adult education. He is a regular columnist for THE IDAHO STATESMAN of Boise, Idaho.

ABOUT THE ARTIST

Julie Wawirka was born July 12, 1954 in Evanston, Illinois and spent her childhood in the suburbs of Chicago. Feeling the urge to go West, she moved to Long Valley, Idaho in 1978. Her work has been shown in the Boise Gallery of Art and the Museum of American Art, the Smithsonian Institute, Washington, D.C.